Contents

Preface

"What would Jesus do?" is the central question of Charles Sheldon's famous novel *In His Steps*. It seems appropriate to offer some reflections on this important question on the one hundredth anniversary of that novel's puublication. It is wonderful that many Christian youth are now wearing bracelets, necklaces, and pins with the letters WWJD. Could it be that God is moving us toward a spiritual revival by drawing us back to this basic question?

This book is the accumulation of a series of sermons which were preached through the summer of 1997. In the past, I have taken sermons and Bible class lectures and edited them into books. Some of these books are used as texts for Bible students who wish to become lay pastors. Others are written for general encouragement and inspiration. In these previous books, the text was not left in its original form as delivered to our congregation, but significantly edited into its final written version. This current book is different in the fact that each chapter, while edited, is presented in its original sermon format.

The motivation for publishing this book is two fold. First, we believe that what we have found helpful in our church can be helpful to others. Second, all of the profits from this book are going to help build a local Habitat for Humanity home.

My thanks to Prescott Area Habitat for Humanity for funding this project. I thank Donna Lange for her many hours of detailed editing. Thanks go to our church staff, Kathy, Sam, Denise, Chuck, and Wayne, who help me find time to write while they cover the daily ministry of our church. A special thanks to Bob, Linda, and Mark of Educational Ministries for their wisdom and encouragement in the details of producing this book. Finally, thanks to my wife and children for giving me permission to share stories from our personal lives in the belief that intimate experiences often teach universal truths.

Bruce Humphrey
Prescott, Arizona
October 29, 1997

In His Steps: Part I

Then he said to them all, "If any want to become my followers, let them deny themselves and take up their cross daily and follow me. For those who want to save their life will lose it, and those who lose their life for my sake will save it. What does it profit them if they gain the whole world, but lose or forfeit themselves? Those who are ashamed of me and of my words, of them the Son of Man will be ashamed when he comes in his glory and the glory of the Father and of the holy angels."

Luke 9:23-26 NRSV

While we were staying for some days, a prophet named Agabus came down from Judea. And coming to us he took Paul's girdle and bound his own feet and hands, and said, "Thus says the Holy Spirit, 'So shall the Jews at Jerusalem bind the man who owns his girdle and deliver him into the hands of the Gentiles.' '' When we heard this, we and the people there begged him not to go up to Jerusalem. Then Paul answered, "What are you doing, weeping and breaking my heart? For I am ready not only to be imprisoned but even to die at Jerusalem for the name of the Lord Jesus." And when he would not be persuaded, we ceased and said, "The will of the Lord be done."

Acts 21:10-14

One of the things I enjoy about summertime is the extra time for reading. When the pace slows slightly and the sunlight lasts longer, we seem to have some extra time to read. One of my favorite aspects of summertime during my school days was when I could lie in the sun beside a swimming pool and read. Have you made up your summer reading list yet? If not, I recommend your including a novel by Charles Sheldon called *In His Steps*. I have read it three times over the last ten years. I still find its ideas challenging.

A little girl wrote a letter to God. She wrote, "Dear God, I read your book and I liked it. Did you write any others? I hope to write a book someday with the same kind of stories as yours. Where did you get your ideas? Love, Sara."

I have a pretty good idea where Charles Sheldon got his ideas for the classic Christian novel *In His Steps*. This book could be considered a modern sequel to the book of Acts in the New Testament. Just as the book of Acts ends with the Apostle Paul's paying the price of following Jesus, so the characters in the novel realize that being a disciple of Jesus today is costly.

Jesus never said that following him would be easy. In fact, he often said the opposite. He told parables about the importance of counting the cost before starting on the road to discipleship. He reminded his disciples that following him would lead them to take up their own crosses.

The Apostle Paul was reminded in several ways that if he returned to Jerusalem, he would pay a dear price. He was warned that he would be treated in the same way that Jesus had been treated. He would be bound and handed over to the gentiles. Yet Paul rejected the option of running and hiding. Instead, he insisted on walking in the footsteps of Jesus.

Are we ready to follow Jesus even if it means we will suffer? Do we really want to be his disciples if it means that we must pay the cost of discipleship? Do we really mean it when we say "the Lord's will be done"?

One hundred years ago Charles Sheldon published his classic sequel to the book of Acts. Published in 1897, this book would become a bestseller. From the turn of the century to the 1950's, this book sold more copies than any other book with the exception of the Bible itself. This book dominated our American culture.

Yet today there are many who have never even heard of the book *In His Steps*. My wife once referred to this modern classic while taking a college class. The professor had been espousing the philosophy of secular existentialism as being the most helpful, ethical system since World War II. Following class, Kathy asked the teacher's thoughts on the Christian existentialism presented in the book *In His Steps.* The professor responded that she had never even heard of this novel.

How could it be that a book that has sold more than fifteen million copies and was a bestseller for nearly sixty years is now barely known? How is it that this book is no longer stocked in popular book stores? Why has it disappeared from the shelves of our libraries? The answer is more than the fact that the story is somewhat dated. I suspect it has to do with the decadence of our entire society. The ideas presented in this novel fly in the face of what has come to be accepted as normal in our world. Thinking back to the decadence of our society during the "gay 90's," I would suggest that *In His Steps* is as relevant to our modern world as it was a hundred years ago.

While one could summarize the central theme of the book as the cost of being a disciple of Jesus, I think it worth my time this morning to do a book review for those who do not recall the story. If my book review stirs some curiosity so that some of us include it in our summer reading, I will have accomplished my purpose.

The book begins by focusing on the ministry of Reverend Henry Maxwell. He is a well-educated, popular preacher. His preaching has attracted the prominent citizens to his parish the First Church of Raymond. Sunday after Sunday the church is packed as this outstanding preacher delivers his grammatically perfect, oratorical sermons. The featured singer in the choir, Miss Rachel Winslow, has such a beautiful voice, that she has been offered a contract to travel with a leading opera company. Among the leading citizens sitting in the pews are the local newspaper editor, college president, and members of the wealthiest family in town.

Sunday morning Reverend Maxwell preaches a sermon with a text from 1 Peter about following in the footsteps of Jesus. The preacher says that Christians ought not only believe in Jesus' death but also seek to imitate Jesus' life. When the sermon is concluded and the congregation prepares to listen to the choral benediction, something unusual happens. A polite stranger stands in the middle of the sanctuary, not to criticize the sermon, but rather to ask for clarification as to its application.

The stranger is unshaven and unwashed. He explains that he has lost his job and has come to this town looking for work. He reminds the congregation of what the pastor has just said in the sermon. "I was wondering, as I sat there under the gallery, if what you call following Jesus is the same thing as what he taught. What did he mean when he said: 'Follow me!...' What do you Christians mean by following the steps of Jesus?"[1]

The stranger collapses on the carpet beside the communion table. Reverend Maxwell quickly announces that the service is concluded. A doctor rushes forward to help the young man, who is lying on the floor. The stranger is carried over to the pastor's home where he dies six days later. This entire experience dramatically changes the pastor.

The following Sunday Reverend Maxwell stands in his pulpit and announces the death of the stranger. He uses the event to challenge the congregation whether we as Christians are truly living as Christ intended. He repeats the stranger's question, "What does following Jesus mean?" Then the preacher concludes his sermon with the following challenge: "I will put my proposition very plainly, perhaps bluntly. I want volunteers from the First Church who will pledge themselves, earnestly and honestly for an entire year, not to do anything without first asking the question, 'What would Jesus do?' And after asking that question, each one will follow Jesus as exactly as he knows how, no matter what the result may be."[2]

Those wishing to make the commitment are invited to meet in an adjoining room following the service. The pastor is surprised that nearly fifty people decide to take the vow. Among them are the newspaper editor and college president. The wonderful singer Rachel Winslow and her friend Virginia from the wealthiest family are also in the group who want to try this new life.

Edward Norman, the editor of the *Daily News* is the first to put this new style of living to the test. The very next morning, as he reviews the material ready to go to print for the Monday afternoon edition, he spots the article about the prize fight. He pauses and prays about whether Jesus would run such an article glorifying violence. He decides to pull the article. The immediate result is that several paperboys complain that men refused to buy the paper without this article.

Within a few weeks Edward Norman decides that Jesus would not run a Sunday edition of the paper. Thus, he loses more subscribers. He makes the decision to stop advertising tobacco and alcohol products, making those companies angry. When he decides to write his editorials from a strictly Christian nonpartisan ethical viewpoint, rather than supporting his own traditional political party, he loses so many subscribers that the paper is in danger of folding. By the middle of the book he has to ask a fellow Christian for financial assistance to continue publishing the paper as Jesus would.

Rachel Winslow, the singer who has been offered an opera contract, decides that Jesus would want her to share her voice with the less fortunate. She turns down the contract and begins singing at the camp meetings in the seedy part of town. The response is that the tent meetings become filled with people who need Jesus Christ as Lord.

Virginia Page quits her former life of highbrow entertainment and country-club lifestyle so that she can help the poor. She accompanies Rachel to the tent meetings and finds herself befriending a woman of the streets. When the woman is injured in a bar brawl, Virginia opens her own home to nurse the young woman back to health. Virginia's grandmother is so offended that such a woman would be brought to the Page's home that she moves away in embarrassment.

Donald Marsh, the college president, decides that he needs to move beyond the academic halls to become involved in the politics of the town. He decides to run for office on a ticket which promises to close the local taverns and establish an alcohol-free community. The political battle embroils him in the experience of being slandered. His reputation is questioned, and he even finds himself being physically assaulted for his views.

These are just a few of the examples which Sheldon presents as he plays with the idea of what would happen if we took Jesus seriously in his call to follow in his steps. The pastor himself finds that it is expensive to act as Jesus would even when it comes to preaching and leading a church. He takes on the challenge of leaving his comfortable pulpit to guest preach at the tent meeting across town. Reverend Maxwell has never before tried to preach to a crowd of doubters and hecklers. He realizes humbly that his oratorical style leaves something to be desired when presenting the gospel to people from different backgrounds. Many of his own church members become upset that his preaching is becoming more down-to-earth and practical; therefore, they leave the church.

Of course, this is just a novel. It has no basis in fact. It is dated to the nineteenth century temperance debates. Surely it has no relevance today. Then again, maybe it does.

Just as history tends to cycle, I wonder if we are not seeing similar decadence as that which our culture faced at the end of the nineteenth century. The prominent anti-Christian philosophy of that day was utilitarianism. Utilitarianism taught people to make ethical decisions based on what would help the most people. Arguing that there was no absolute standard for moral conduct, the best that non-religious philosophers could offer was a subjective standard of what seemed to work for the benefit of most.

Following World War II, we saw the rise of the non-religious philosophy called secular existentialism. This philosophy taught people to make moral decisions based on whether they felt the world would be better if everyone made the same decision in a comparable situation. This situational approach argued that there were no absolutes or standards on which we can base our lives.

These two philosophies sound strangely similar. Much of nineteenth century utilitarianism has become twentieth century secular existentialism. These philosophies do not believe that there are any objective standards for ethical and moral conduct. The central problem in these two philosophical systems is that they rely on the individual to make decisions for the benefit of others without taking into account our amazing tendency to make our decisions based on what benefits us the most. There is no room for sinful selfishness in either of these two philosophies.

Comic author Patrick McManus has put his finger on the flaw in the reasoning of secular ethics. He writes about situational ethics as follows: "Situation: Suppose you are mountain climbing and your partner, with whom you are roped together, slips and falls. He jerks you into space with him. The two of you are suspended from the rope with him on the bottom end. You could climb up the rope, but you can't climb up dragging your partner behind you. If you cut the rope beneath you, your partner falls. If you don't cut the rope, both of you will freeze to death. The ethical question: Should you cut the rope and save yourself, even as your partner watches in horror, or should you say, 'Hey, look, Fred, a bald eagle!' " [3]

The problem with situational ethics as they have been presented in the secular philosophies is that they do not take seriously our human sinfulness. We will choose to cut the rope and save ourselves one way or the other. The only ethical question becomes whether or not to distract our partner while cutting the rope and saving ourselves.

Our Christian basis for moral and ethical thinking differs markedly from those non-religious philosophies. Our response to such thinking was summarized by Charles Sheldon's *In His Steps*. As Christians, our absolute standard of conduct is the life of our Lord. What is morally right is whatever Jesus would do. What is morally wrong is whatever Jesus would not do. Jesus, the perfect human being, has set the absolute standards for us. Following in the steps of Jesus gives us a basis for making difficult moral choices in a world of gray areas.

Imagine what could happen in our society if we Christians asked ourselves, disregarding whatever personal sacrifice it might cost, "What would Jesus do?" and then sought to do it. Imagine what would happen in our political climate if people disregarded their party allegiances and simply sought to make every political decision based on what Jesus would do. Imagine what would happen in our court systems if attorneys and judges were guided entirely by the thought of what Jesus would do. Imagine what would happen in our churches if pastors led their churches as they believed Jesus would, regardless of the cost.

Of course, there is a serious flaw in this approach. For us to really live this way, we need something I have not even mentioned today, something we will consider next week.

---

[1] Charles M. Sheldon, *In His Steps* (New York: The World's Popular Classics Books, Inc., 1897) 9.

[2] Ibid. 15.

[3] Patrick F. McManus, *How I Got This Way* (New York: Henry Holt and Company, 1994) 35.

In His Steps: Part II

And one of the crowd answered him, "Teacher, I brought my son to you, for he has a dumb spirit; and wherever it seizes him, it dashes him down; and he foams and grinds his teeth and becomes rigid; and I asked your disciples to cast it out, and they were not able." And he answered them, "O faithless generation, how long am I to be with you? How long am I to bear with you? Bring him to me." And they brought the boy to him; and when the spirit saw him, immediately it convulsed the boy, and he fell on the ground and rolled about, foaming at the mouth. And Jesus asked his father, "How long has he had this?" And he said, "From childhood. And it has often cast him into the fire and into the water, to destroy him; but if you can do anything, have pity on us and help us." And Jesus said to him, "If you can! All things are possible to him who believes." Immediately the father of the child cried out and said, "I believe; help my unbelief!" And when Jesus saw that a crowd came running together, he rubuked the unclean spirit, saying to it, "You dumb and deaf spirit, I command you, come out of him, and never enter him again." And after crying out and convulsing him terribly, it came out, and the boy was like a corpse; so that most of them said, "He is dead." But Jesus took him by the hand and lifted him up, and he arose. And when he had entered the house, his disciples asked him privately, "Why could we not cast it out?" And he said to them, "This kind cannot be driven out by anything but prayer."

Mark 9:17-29

Bless the Lord, O my soul;
and all that is within me, bless his holy name!

Psalm 103:1

I am pleased to hear that many in our church have purchased or ordered the book *In His Steps*. Last week we learned that this book was the bestselling novel in America for almost sixty years. Yet many in our day have never read it. I encouraged us to consider including this book on our summer reading list. Apparently many took me seriously.

When I preached the first part of this message last week, I did not know that Paul Harvey had recently told a story of a graduating class which was wearing wrist bracelets inscribed with the letters W.W.J.D. Last Friday night's Phoenix news on TV reported that more and more Christian teens are wearing these bracelets. Wearing bracelets with the inscription W.W.J.D. is becoming a fad. The letters are intended to remind the wearer to consider the question: **What would Jesus do?** This was the central question from the novel *In His Steps*. We concluded last week's sermon by realizing that if we Christians used this approach to make our moral and ethical choices, it might have very positive effects in our society. On the other hand, I suggested at the close of last week's message that there is a serious flaw in this approach.

The flaw is not simply the realization that different personalities will come to different decisions in the same situation. This thought was the focus of last Sunday evening's discussion following the message. In fact, the novel does a masterful job of pointing out that Christians of different personalities and backgrounds may come to different decisions about what Jesus would do in their situation. Thus, we need to avoid the simplistic view that there is only one right, moral answer in each situation.

For instance, after last Sunday's evening service one of our youth pointed out that a person who has been blessed with a beautiful musical voice may still be faithful to Christ while touring with an opera company. Even though Rachel Winslow chose to remain in the small town and sing for the local evangelistic tent meetings, it does not mean that it might not be possible for someone else to travel with the opera company and be a witness for Jesus on the road.

The flaw in this approach is its underlying assumption. Before we can answer the question: What would Jesus do?, we must be close enough to Jesus to know his heart. It does little good when we find ourselves in a moral dilemma to wonder what Jesus would do if we have not taken time to know Jesus beforehand. If we have not prepared ourselves ahead of time through a deep relationship with Jesus, we will not be able to discern the answer even though it is still the right question.

Several of the characters in the book realize that simply asking the right question does not assure that Christian people will come to the right decision. Let me quote a portion of the book. The context is a discussion of whether the newspaper ought to draw on the financial resources of fellow Christians in order to continue publishing. The editor of the paper acknowledges that he will likely make some mistakes in his choices about what Jesus would do. The wealthy woman who is offering to help the paper out of its financial problems responds, "I think we are beginning to understand the meaning of that command, 'Grow in the grace and knowledge of our Lord and Saviour Jesus Christ.' I am sure I do not know all that he would do in detail until I know him better."

The pastor then comments, "That is very true. I am beginning to understand that I cannot interpret the probable action of Jesus until I know better what his spirit is. We must know Jesus before we can imitate him."[1]

Realizing that the answer to the question requires a deeper knowledge of the heart of Jesus, how do we get this knowledge? This is the question for our consideration today.

I do not do well when watching the popular TV show *Jeopardy.* I frequently feel pretty stupid. Perhaps this is the reason I enjoyed a comedian's description of a person playing on *Jeopardy* for the first time. The announcer read the card with the answer. "This fruit is long and yellow and must be pealed in order to be eaten." One player pushed his button ahead of the other contestants. He called out the answer, "Banana!" The announcer responded,

"I'm sorry, but you must word your response as a question." The player thought for a moment and then responded again, "Banana?"

When a *Jeopardy* player gets the question right, he receives points. When Christians get the question right, it can start us on the path to becoming the person God wants us to be. However, if all we do is get the question right, we will not go very far in imitating Jesus Christ. Being a Christian involves not only asking the right question, it also involves finding the best answer.

Last week we reflected on the idea that there is an absolute standard for ethical and moral decision making in our world of gray areas. The absolute standard for a Christian is the life of Jesus Christ. Since Jesus lived a sinless, perfect life, we can use his life as our standard. One way to do this is to ask the question, "What would Jesus do?"

Michael Jordan and the Chicago Bulls are headed to the playoffs for another national championship. Of course, many young basketball players would love to play like Michael Jordan. Little Johnny watches Michael Jordan in these playoffs and goes to bed dreaming of being as good a player as Jordan. Johnny memorizes the way Michael Jordan dribbles the ball. He admires the way Michael Jordan drives to the basket and is in awe of Jordan's hang time. "What would Michael Jordan do?" Johnny asks as he dribbles the ball toward the basket. This is fine as far as it goes. But becoming like Michael Jordan will take more than simply asking what Jordan would do during the game. It takes lots of practice between games.

Parents of an aspiring basketball player teach their child that there is more to the sport than simply playing the game. Becoming an athlete involves daily disciplines. The young athlete is told by his coach to do push-ups and run every day. Weightlifting and sit-ups are part of the daily regimen in order to become an outstanding athlete. Natural talent and genuine desire are not enough to make a young person into a professional athlete. Becoming like Michael Jordan takes daily discipline.

The first time little Mary heard the music of Andrew Lloyd Webber, she wanted to grow up to become like him. She dreamed of writing music as stirring and majestic as Webber's. She dreamed of directing a huge orchestra which would be playing her musical pieces.

It is fine to dream of becoming the best. However, we know that little Mary will have to take years of music lessons. She will have to start with playing the scales and learning how to read music. No matter how talented Mary may be, she will need to develop daily musical routines to become outstanding in her musical abilities. There is no shortcut to greatness. Becoming great in any field involves daily discipline.

The same is true for Christians learning to follow Jesus. We would be foolish to think that we could answer the question: What would Jesus do? without needing to practice some daily disciplines that taught us to become more like Jesus.

The novel *In His Steps* does a good job of pointing to this important truth. Soon after the group of fifty church members take their vow to try and live this way for a year, they realize that it will be important to continue meeting regularly to help each other. The discipline of regular fellowship becomes a new part of their weekly activities. They start staying after church each Sunday to discuss their current struggles to live by the standard of what Jesus would do.

Individuals who are trying to live by this new standard find themselves more involved with prayer. Several times in the book the author describes someone on his knees seeking to know what Christ would do in his particular situation. The discipline of prayer must undergird this approach to Christian living.

Other disciplines such as simplicity, solitude, giving, and service are each given some import in the novel. By the end of the novel one realizes that this question, "What would Jesus do?" is much more complex than it sounds at first. It is really the call to a new kind of life which involves many new spiritual disciplines.

Years ago Richard Foster wrote a wonderful, nonfiction book about twelve of the basic spiritual disciplines of Christianity. His book *Celebration of Discipline* has challenged me to draw nearer to Christ through some practical, daily, weekly, and monthly routines. Foster reminds the reader that we cannot make our spirits grow any more than a farmer can force a seed to grow. However, just as a farmer can create a positive environment for growth by weeding the field, and by fertilizing and watering the seed, so we can create a positive environment for our spirits to grow. We create the right environment to nurture the spirit by practicing daily spiritual disciplines. The spiritual disciplines such as prayer and fellowship, worship and Bible study, create an open heart which God can mold to make more Christlike .[2]

The gospel lesson today recalls a time when the disciples could not help a man with a sick son. When Jesus arrived on the scene, he diagnosed the cause of the problem as a demon and thus cast the demon out of the boy. Later, after the boy was healed, the disciples wondered what they had done wrong. "Why could we not drive the demon out?" Jesus answered, "This kind comes out only through prayer."

How was Jesus able to handle the healing need? Jesus had practiced regular disciplined prayer before he ever faced the situation. How do we face comparable situations where we discover someone is in genuine need for God to touch and change them? Before we ask what Jesus would do, we need to practice the disciplines that Jesus practiced: prayer, solitude, fellowship, worship, scripture study, and meditation, to name a few.

This week I talked with someone who was struggling with an issue of forgiveness. She commented, "What would Jesus do? I guess he would forgive. But I am not ready to forgive. I can't forgive!" I believe her. I think it is absolutely impossible for her to forgive right now. However, I believe with some developing of the spiritual disciplines, she would find herself able to do what Jesus would do over the next few months.

Years ago I met with a pastor's wife. As we prayed together, I recall her bitterness toward some of the elders of the church. She told me that she was wrong to hold her bitterness toward some of these elders, but she felt unable to be as forgiving as Jesus would be. She knew what Jesus would do in the situation, but she was simply unable to do it.

Her story recalled the night her son prepared to join the church. He, along with other young people of the church, had completed the communicant's class. It was the night to meet with the elders in order to be voted into church membership. Her son was so proud to be joining his father's church. She watched as the boy checked his tie three or four times to be sure it was tied right and hung straight. She hugged him as he headed out the front door and heard him call back, "Pray for me, Mom." She encouraged him with her motherly words, "You will do fine." Thus, their seventh-grade son went to the meeting to become a church member.

Later that night her husband returned home and was obviously upset. She pried the news out of him as to what had happened at the elders' meeting. After the children had left the room, some of the elders criticized the pastor's son as being too immature to join yet. They questioned whether the boy really understood what Christianity meant. I do not recall whether they actually voted not to receive the boy into membership or whether the parents were simply hurt over the criticisms. I do recall that this pastor's wife was weeping as she finished telling me the cause of her bitterness toward those elders. She blamed the elders for her son's rejection of the church.

Was she justified in her anger? Of course she was! Can we understand why she would find it so hard to forgive? Surely we can see how deeply hurt she would be. I am sure most secular counselors would dismiss her bitterness as a legitimate form of expressing her pain in that situation. However, she really wanted to have the correct, godly attitudes that a Christian ought to have. She wanted to be more like Christ; she just did not know how to get there. So we started practicing the discipline of prayer together. We prayed that God would touch the hearts of those elders and draw them close to Jesus Christ. We prayed that those elders would become a blessing to her husband's ministry. We prayed that God move throughout the church in ways that draw people closer.

As she prayed with me week after week, we began to notice together that her heart was releasing her bitterness. After months of disciplined prayer I could tell a real difference in her attitudes toward the elders. She could not change herself. She could not make the bitterness go away. But she could pray. Through the discipline of prayer God changed her heart.

21

The key to the spiritual disciplines is understanding the difference between God's responsibility and ours. We are to be responsible in practicing the spiritual disciplines. God is to be responsible for changing our hearts. The end result is that we find ourselves becoming more like Jesus. We become people who walk in his steps.

Some years ago I visited one of our members and heard that she had had a terrible Christmas. She spent Christmas day throwing herself a pity party. "Nobody called me. Everybody was too busy with their own families and Christmas dinners to think of me." She wallowed in her loneliness and self-pity. After listening for a while, I finally challenged her to try a spiritual discipline. I asked her to try calling a person lonelier than she was. I suggested that she phone someone who is homebound and just be a friend.

By the next Christmas she had developed the discipline of service. She was in the regular habit of calling people each week and sending uplifting cards to cheer up people who could not get out of their houses. I recall seeing her after the next Christmas and asking, "How was your Christmas?" She gushed with enthusiasm. "I had a wonderful day! I went to a nursing home to visit a shut-in on Christmas day. I also took someone out for a nice Christmas lunch."

God had changed her heart, replacing the sorrow of self-pity with the joy of service. She was like a different person. How did she become more like Christ? She learned to practice one of the spiritual disciplines.

Sometimes, when I am down, I practice the discipline of personal worship. I know myself well enough to know that I can tend toward pity parties myself. When I am down, I have let little things get to me. I let everything get out of perspective. I can relate to the psalmist in Psalm 103. The writer does not feel like praising God, but he takes his soul by the scruff of the neck and forces himself to praise the Lord anyway. "Praise the Lord, oh my soul!"

While driving the car, I put in a tape of praise music and turn the volume up to loud. Pretty soon I start tapping my foot (not the one on the accelerator). Next, I join in singing the songs of praise at the top of my voice. Driving down the highway, I probably look a little silly bobbing my head and singing loudly with the praise music. However, I find myself restored to joy in the Lord. It is amazing how often I move easily from loud praise music into a quiet prayer time. Soon I feel surrounded by God's amazing love.

What would Jesus do? This is the right question for those seeking to follow the Lord. The problem is that we will not discern the best answer until we know Jesus intimately.

---

[1] Charles M. Sheldon, *In His Steps* (New York: The World's Popular Classics Books, Inc., 1897) 136.

[2] Richard Foster, *Celebration of Discipline* (San Francisco: Harper and Row, 1978) 6.

The Discipline of Meditation

Then Jesus was led up by the Spirit into the wilderness to be tempted by the devil. And he fasted forty days and forty nights, and afterward he was hungry. And the tempter came and said to him, "If you are the Son of God, command these stones to become loaves of bread." But he answered, "It is written 'Man shall not live by bread alone, but by every word that proceeds from the mouth of God.' " Then the devil took him to the holy city, and set him on the pinnacle of the temple, and said to him, "If you are the Son of God, throw yourself down; for it is written, 'He will give his angels charge of you' and 'On their hands they will bear you up, lest you strike your foot against a stone.' " Jesus said to him, "Again it is written, 'You shall not tempt the Lord your God.' " Again, the devil took him to a very high mountain, and showed him all the kingdoms of the world and the glory of them; and he said to him, "All these I will give you, if you will fall down and worship me." Then Jesus said to him, "Begone, Satan! for it is written 'You shall worship the Lord your God and him only shall you serve.' " Then the devil left him, and behold, angels came and ministered to him.

Matthew 4:1-11

Blessed is the man
  who walks not in the counsel of the wicked,
nor stands in the way of sinners,
  nor sits in the seat of scoffers;

but his delight is in the law of the Lord,
and on his law he meditates day and night.

Psalm 1:1-2

What would Jesus do? Before we can answer this question in our specific situations, we need to learn the spiritual disciplines which Jesus practiced. Let us consider the discipline of meditation.

It was one of those days. Nothing seemed to be going right. When he ended up in the hospital, he carefully wrote out his request for sick leave as follows:

When I got to the building, I found that the hurricane had knocked some bricks off the top. So I rigged up a beam with a pulley at the top of the building and hoisted up a couple of barrels full of bricks. When I had fixed the building there were a lot of bricks left over. I loaded all of them into the barrel and then went to the bottom of the building and cast off the line. Unfortunately the barrel of bricks was heavier than I was and before I knew what was happening, the barrel started down, jerking me off the ground. I decided to hang on. Halfway up I met the barrel coming down and received a hard blow on the shoulder. I then continued to the top, banging my head against the beam and getting my fingers jammed in the pulley. When the barrel hit the ground, it burst it's bottom, allowing all the bricks to spill out. I was now heavier than the barrel and so started down again at a high speed. Halfway down I met the barrel coming up and received more injuries to my shins. When I hit the ground, I landed on the bricks, getting several painful cuts. At this point I must have lost my presence of mind because I let go of the line. The barrel came down, giving me another heavy blow on the head and putting me in the hospital.[1]

If we can picture this situation in our minds, we have what it takes to be successful in the discipline of Christian meditation. It takes imagination to practice this discipline. While we all had plenty of imagination as children, sadly many of us as adults stop using our imaginations. Imagination is one God-given way to make the Scriptures come alive.

Unfortunately when some people hear the word *meditation,* they think immediately of Eastern religions and cults, which teach something quite foreign to Christian discipline. While meditation as practiced in many New Age teachings involves emptying the mind, Christian meditation involves filling the mind. We renew our minds through the intertwining of imagination with the Bible.

Jesus must have meditated on Scripture during his forty-day fast in the wilderness. We often think of this Bible story as an example of Satan's attacking Jesus just when Jesus was at his weakest moment. After forty days of hunger and isolation, surely Jesus must have needed food and conversation. Perhaps we have misunderstood this account of the beginning of Jesus' ministry.

From the way that Jesus answered the temptations of the Devil, it is apparent that Jesus was armed with the scriptures. Jesus answered each temptation by quoting a relevant biblical text. I suspect that rather than Jesus being at his weakest, he was actually at his strongest. He had just practiced several of the spiritual disciplines: fasting, prayer, meditation on scripture, and solitude. Perhaps the reason God allowed the Devil to tempt Jesus with the most difficult temptations was that Jesus was better prepared after the forty days in the wilderness than at any other time.

Will we be ready for the next temptations that come our way? We will if we regularly maintain the same spiritual disciplines Jesus practiced.

Recent surveys show that as few as eleven percent of Americans read the Bible every day. More than half of Americans do not read the Bible even once a month. Among Christians the statistics are not much better. Among those who are active in their Christian faith, only eighteen percent claim to read their Bibles every day. Sadly nearly one fourth of Christians admit they never read their Bibles.[2]

There is too little Bible reading today. If these are the statistics for Bible reading, imagine what the statistics are for meditation on the Scriptures. The difference between Bible reading and meditation is like the difference between making tea by dipping a tea bag only once into hot water as opposed to letting it steep for several minutes. Unfortunately when it comes to letting God's Word influence us, most of us are satisfied to simply have the tea bag dipped once on Sunday mornings and then wonder why we struggle with our faith. We need to learn how to let God's Word steep in our hearts so that we grow into an intimate relationship with Jesus Christ.

Meditation is more than simply Bible reading. It is also different from Bible study. One of the problems with Bible study is that it can become too academic and sterile. It is possible to read the letters of Paul or the prophecies of Jeremiah without any personal sense of involvement. Meditation helps the Bible come alive by inviting us to bring our own feelings into the text. The goal of meditation is to discover within our own hearts the feelings which the Bible characters felt. The facts of their experiences may be different from what we have experienced, yet our feelings about the experiences can still be the same.

Michael Lindvall, a Presbyterian pastor and author, tells the story of a father who cannot understand how his first-grade son has such difficulties in reading. The father is horrified that the first-grade teacher is recommending holding the child back due to reading problems. He is astounded that his son does not enjoy reading as much as he does. School has always been easy for this pastor with a master's degree. He decides his son must not be trying hard enough, so he makes a personal commitment to work with his son every day through the summer.

Practicing reading was agony for both father and son. Grammar rules were explained over and over. The father's tone of voice became more tense and impatient as his son's progress was so slow. The words on the page seemed a mystery to the boy. Many summer reading sessions ended with an angry father and a son in tears. By the end of the summer their relationship was severely strained.

An opportunity for reconciliation of father and son occurred through the local, end-of-summer, radio-sponsored treasure hunt. Chris asked his dad to participate with him on the daily radio treasure hunt. Each morning for one week in August the eight a.m. radio broadcast included a clue for children to search for a treasure.

Monday morning father and son sit in the kitchen listening to the first clue. After they figure out the clue, they drive to that part of town where the clue is fulfilled. By the time they arrive on Monday, there are already thirty-five other children at the sight, and somebody has found the treasure. The next morning they wait for the second clue, only to be beaten to the spot by others. The same thing happens on Wednesday and Thursday. Even though they have not captured the treasure, at least father and son are happily attempting the hunt together.

Friday morning they climb into the car and turn on the engine. They wait for the clue with the car in gear, ready to race down the street. As soon as the clue comes on, father and son consult with each other. Dad has it figured out. It's a cornfield on the edge of town!

They pull up to the cornfield and rejoice that there are no other cars. The father jumps out of the car and grabs his son's hand. They start running up and down the edge of the cornfield. When they cannot spot the treasure, they change their plan. Convinced that the treasure must be hidden on the small hill in the middle of the cornfield, the father tells his son to stay with the car while he wanders into the seven foot high cornstalks.

Once in the midst of the tall, ready-to-be-harvested corn, the father feels like he is walking through a jungle. He follows the straight row of corn until it ends with a new row of corn planted at an angle to the first row. He walks along the second row until he thinks he may be walking parallel to the hill. He cuts across a few rows of corn and catches another row planted at a forty-five-degree angle to the row he is walking.

Forty-five minutes later the father gives up and decides to head back to the car. He turns right and then left but without the aid of sunlight he realizes that all the cornstalks look alike. The rows have no distinguishing features. He realizes he is lost in the cornfield. He can't find the car.

Several minutes go by as the father begins to worry about his son, abandoned on the side of the road. He worries that others will wonder what kind of father leaves a seven-year-old boy alone. He figures other treasure hunters have arrived and found the child crying. They have probably called the police by now. When he wanders out of the cornfield, the police officer will radio the news to the worried mother and the headlines the following morning will tell the story of how he abandoned his son on the side of the road.

Just as the father's fears hit their worst scenario, he hears a car horn honking. Someone is helping him get his direction by sounding short blasts on the horn. By the time he follows the noise, he comes out of the cornfield nearly a quarter of a mile beyond the car. As he approaches the vehicle, he discovers his son is alone, honking the horn. With relief, his son jumps from the car and runs to him, shouting, "Dad, I found you!"

The treasure has been found by someone else. On the way home father and son decide not to tell Mom what has happened. However, Dad realizes something as he looks at his son. The same way he felt when he was lost in the cornfield is how his son feels when he is wading through unfamiliar letters on a page. One has never been lost in a cornfield; the other has never had trouble with school. While the facts of their lives are totally different, the feelings of fear and confusion, frustration and disorientation are the same.[3]

Have we ever felt confused and bewildered? If we have, we can use these feelings we have had to meditate on Bible passages. While we were not with Jesus in the garden the night of his arrest, we know something of what the disciples must have felt as they melted into the shadows in confusion and fear. We can use our feelings of confusion and disorientation to meditate on the resurrection stories. We have felt the kind of confusion and fear that the women who arrived at the tomb on Easter morning felt. We can even use this familiar feeling to meditate on the place in 2 Peter where he describes Paul's letters as "hard to understand" (2 Peter 3:16).

Meditation on the Scriptures involves taking our familiar feelings and reading them into the unfamiliar experiences of Bible characters. The facts of our lives and the lives of Bible characters may be totally different. Yet the feelings can be very similar. This is the power of meditation. It takes what we know and helps us better understand what we do not know.

The sad thing about meditation is that we often found it easy to do as children. Now as adults, we need to rediscover the power of our imaginations to enter into the feelings of the Bible stories.

I recall early in my career arriving home one afternoon to the laughing smile of my wife. She whispered to me that she needed to tell me something that had happened earlier that day. Out of hearing distance from our older son, Kathy told me that Nathan had held a worship service for a group of dolls. She had secretly watched as he lined up the dolls in rows and proceeded to announce the hymns. He repeated the hymn number twice. He asked one of the deacons to receive the offering. He led a short prayer. Then he preached to his doll congregation. His text was the story about Abraham's sacrifice of Isaac. (I had recently preached on this text.) Nathan explained the Bible story to the dolls by reminding them that it is normal for a child to love his father very much. However, there are times when God calls us to sacrifice even what we love the most. According to four-year-old Nathan's version of the story, Isaac argued with God that he did not want to sacrifice his father on the altar. God was unbending. "I know that you love your father very much, but you must sacrifice him as an offering to me." Finally, just as Isaac was preparing to bring the knife down, an angel stopped him and told him that a ram could be substituted in place of his father's life.

This is a wonderful four-year-old's meditation on a classic Bible story! The facts may be slightly altered, but the feelings are very accurate. Sadly, if we are not careful, we will take this imaginative mind with a natural ability to meditate and destroy the sense of wonder by explaining the historic and cultural background of the Bible. If we are not careful, we will take away a child's ability to meditate and exchange it for sterile doctrine and rote memorization.

In the sixteenth century Ignatius of Loyola wrote a book on the spiritual disciplines. He founded a discipleship movement in the Catholic church called the Society of Jesus or Jesuits. When discussing the discipline of meditation, Loyola encouraged

Christians to visualize the Bible story by "application of the senses."[4] Using all five senses, we try to picture in our minds what it would have been like to be in a particular Bible story. We might ask ourselves what smells, sights, sounds, tastes, and textures would have been felt if we had been in the situation described in the Bible.

Some years ago I was meditating on how Jesus must have felt when he was serving the disciples at the Last Supper. He watched as they worried about who got the best seat. He washed their feet as they refused to care for each other. He ate the meal knowing that his betrayer was in the room. He knew that all of them would abandon him. How must it have felt?

As I was meditating on this familiar Bible story, my mind flashed to a memory from my teen years. My senior year of high school our family was selected as the host family for a foreign student. Tao Kay was from Laos. He arrived in August, and we threw a large party for our friends to meet our exchange student. Tao and I quickly became like brothers. Since I had never had a real brother, this was a wonderful time in my life.

We lay awake at night talking about everything. We compared his culture to mine. We laughed a lot. We whispered some of our secrets about romance and feelings for girls. Over the next four months I grew to love this foreign exchange brother. Then it happened.

One night I came home after gymnastics practice to find that Tao Kay had packed his bags. An official representative from the foreign exchange office informed our family that Kay was being moved to another host family. We learned that he had reported our family as not providing decent meals for his needs. It was simply a miscommunication. He had been told by his mother to eat meat every day. When he sat down to our dinner table, he would ask what we were eating. My mom would answer by telling him the names of the various dishes. For instance, she would tell him that we were having pork chops or sausage and sauerkraut or whatever the dish was. While we had been eating plenty of meat dishes, Kay did not hear the word meat, so he thought we were not feeding him properly.

After he left the house, I ran to my room and started to cry. I sobbed into my pillow. At seventeen I felt betrayed and misunderstood. I was hurt and angry. Later Tao Kay and I resolved our hurt feelings and became close friends again and remained so even after he returned to his home country.

Could it be that what I felt that night was a little like what Jesus felt at the Last Supper? Meditations such as this can help the Bible come alive in our hearts.

We need more than a quick dip of the tea bag on Sunday mornings if we are to become more like Jesus. Meditation is more than Bible reading or even Bible study. How long are we letting the tea bag of God's Word steep in our lives?

---

[1] Bob Phillips, *More Good Clean Jokes* (Irvine: Harvest House, 1974) 50.

[2] Donald S. Whitney, *Spiritual Disciplines for the Christian Life* (Colorado Springs: NavPress, 1991) 27-28.

[3] Michael L. Lindvall, *The Good News from North Haven* (New York: Pocket Books 1991) 119-132.

[4] Richard J. Foster, *Celebration of Discipline: The Path to Spiritual Growth* (San Francisco: Harper and Row, 1978) 22.

The Discipline of Study

And God gave Solomon wisdom and understanding beyond measure, and largeness of mind like the sand on the seashore, so that Solomon's wisdom surpassed the wisdom of all the people of the east, and all the wisdom of Egypt. For he was wiser than all other men, wiser than Eihan the Ezrahite, and Heman, Calcol, and Darda, the sons of Mahol; and his fame was in all the nations round about.

He also uttered three thousand proverbs; and his songs were a thousand and five. He spoke of trees, from the cedar that is in Lebanon to the hyssop that grows out of the wall; he spoke also of beasts, and of birds, and of reptiles, and of fish. And men came from all peoples to hear the wisdom of Solomon, and from all the kings of the earth, who had heard of his wisdom.

1 Kings 4:29-34

Do your best to present yourself to God as one approved, a workman who has no need to be ashamed, rightly handling the word of truth.

2 Timothy 2:15

The Bible tells us that King Solomon was the wisest person of his day. People from other countries came to Jerusalem to listen to King Solomon's wisdom. How did he become so wise? Yes, we know King Solomon prayed and asked God for wisdom (1 Kings 3). However, just praying about it was not enough. The Bible follows the prayer for wisdom with the very next chapter's describing King Solomon's spiritual discipline of study.

King Solomon was a lifelong student. He examined plant life and carefully watched animal behaviors. He studied birds and fish. Through the spiritual discipline of study King Solomon learned to reflect on what he had seen. The end result was that he grew wise.

Wisdom is not the same as the accumulation of information. It is possible to know lots of information and still not be wise. Wisdom comes by combining the discipline of prayer with the discipline of study. Today we want to consider the discipline of study. We can define this discipline as the deepening of insight through paying attention, analyzing information, and then tearing it apart and putting it back together with fresh perspective. We can practice the discipline of study in such areas as science, reading books, observing people, relationships, and of course Scripture.

A wife asked her husband, "Why do you always answer a question with a question?" He responded, "Do I do that?" Jesus, like that husband, frequently answered people's questions by asking them a question in return. Why did Jesus do this? Jesus was teaching people to practice the discipline of study.

While on vacation, our family visited Carlsbad Caverns. We watched one evening as thousands of bats flew from the mouth of the cave. We took an entire day to hike down into the cave and wander through on the guided and unguided tours. I was struck by the names of various stalactite and stalagmite formations. As we entered the cave, the first formations were named by an early explorer with such names as "Devil's Spring," "Devil's Hump," and "Witch's Fingers." The deeper, inner caverns had names such as "King's Palace," and "Queen's Chamber."

One of the forest service guides asked our group if we could guess the progression of thought as Bill White studied the cave over the years. We realized that White's early experiences must have been frightening. Perhaps he feared the cave was leading him into the depths of hell. When White named the structures after devils and witches, he was reflecting his own perceptions about the cave. As he became more confident in his deeper explorations, he grew in respect for the cavernous interior and changed his perceptions as to their danger. Thus, names like "Devil's Hump" gave way to names like "King's Palace." Years of studying the cave helped him change his mind about the cave.

The forest ranger at the evening bat flight asked the crowd what were the common perceptions about bats. People responded with common fears about bats carrying rabies and vampire bats sucking blood through their fangs. The ranger then explained that bats need not be feared. Bats die of rabies just like we do; they simply die a little slower so that they can carry the virus and infect others just as skunks or dogs do. The Mexican fantail bats, native to those caverns, do not feed on human blood, but rather go out at night to feed on insects. Bats are important in the ecological balance of the area. Even the feared vampire bats feed on cow's blood by licking an open wound rather than sucking through their fangs. We learned that recent studies of bats and caves are leading to major breakthroughs in medical areas including a possible cure for cancer.

What happens when we ask questions? The process of searching for answers to our questions leads us into the discipline of study. By studying, we often come to a change in our mind. The biblical word for this is *repentance.* The Greek word *metanioa,* translated as *repent,* actually means *a change of mind.* We become wise by changing our minds through study.

This last week in our Vacation Bible School, I taught the junior high class. Our theme verse for the class was Luke 2:46 where Jesus at age twelve questioned the priests at the temple. Realizing that many of our young people watch lots of video movies through the summer months, I decided to focus the class on learning to question movies and TV. We combined watching portions of popular videos with class analysis of how Hollywood movies distort information. For instance, we interviewed attorneys, fire fighters, and police officers to contrast what they told us about their jobs in the real world with the way movies present these professions. When our youth expected the average police officer to fire his gun at a criminal at least twice a month, since this happens all the time in the movies, we learned that most officers seldom shoot at a criminal. When our youth asked the police officer if he shoots for the leg like in movies, he responded that he has never shot at a criminal's leg. By asking questions, our youth were practicing the discipline of study.

Jesus modeled this discipline when it came to news reports. One day some people reported to Jesus that King Herod had killed some of the Jewish worshipers in Jerusalem (Luke 13:1). Jesus realized that the common interpretation of this event was that the Galileans who were killed must have deserved to die as punishment for something they had done wrong. Instead of accepting this simplistic interpretation of the news, Jesus showed his discipline of study by questioning whether the murdered Galileans were any worse sinners than anyone else (Luke 13:2).

One of my soapbox subjects is my fear that too many people do not practice the discipline of study when it comes to modern news reports. People who watch TV news without practicing the discipline of study can develop distorted perspectives on our society. It is important to remind ourselves that news items catch our attention because they are abnormal. What is normal and ordinary does not get reported since it is common. Only what is unusual and uncommon makes it into the news.

When we hear that a robber has broken into a home in our community, we would be misinterpreting the event if we concluded that all our homes were suddenly in danger of being burglarized. The reason it was in the news was that it was an *unusual* event in our community. When the news reports that something has happened to one home in our community, we need to analyze this information and remind ourselves that nothing has happened to thousands of other homes.

We can practice the spiritual discipline of study when we read magazines. A few months ago I came across a report on the percentage of American homes that are without children. In 1997, according to an April issue of *Newsweek,* approximately 51% of homes in America are without children. Over the next ten years this number will increase to about 58%. Thus, by the year 2005, only approximately 42% of homes will have children. I was reflecting on the fact that my own baby-boomer generation will soon become empty-nest homes. I studied the graph with the article as I reflected on the implications of this information.

I then read the next paragraph. If our society continues at the same divorce rate, by the year 2005 approximately 10% of American homes will have children growing up with a single parent. This leaves about 30% being traditional, two-parent homes. This information coincided with a report I had recently read in a Christian magazine that approximately 80% of children in our society are still growing up in traditional, two-parent families. Therefore, in ten years the number of children growing up in single-parent homes will rise from 20% to about 25%.

How many of us would have guessed that 75-80% of American children are still growing up in traditional, two-parent families? If we do not practice the discipline of study, when we hear news about rising divorce rates, high-risk youth, and rising crime rates, we can easily get the false impression that the majority of our youth are troubled and most families are falling apart. Through the discipline of study we realize that the number of troubled youth and broken families is still a minority in our culture.

It takes the discipline of study not to be swayed by the way Christianity gets treated by the media. Some years ago an article was printed with evidence that the Communist KGB had infiltrated the World Council of Churches' headquarters in Geneva. Some people used this information to withdraw their donations to their local churches. "See, we knew all along that this so-called Christian organization was really a front for Communism!" I did not hear anyone asking the obvious question that arises when we practice the spiritual discipline of study. What was so threatening to the Communists that they felt the need to send KGB spies to infiltrate this organization?

This month the Presbyterian General Assembly voted to further refine the wording of the Fidelity and Chastity Amendment, which was approved last year. Most of us who voted in favor of this amendment last year knew that it needed fine-tuning. We wanted to get it on the books and then refine the wording. Its original wording was more legalistic than most of us wanted, but the intent was the right direction. For instance, if we took it literally as it was approved last year, we would have no room for people to serve as pastors, elders, or deacons who did not maintain absolute rest for the entire Sabbath day, avoiding any form of recreation or work other than to pray and to attend worship (<u>Book of Confessions</u>, pp. 149 and 187).

The wording of last year's amendment said that those who are called to office in the church are to lead a life *"in conformity* to the historic confessional standards of the church." Do we really want to expel from the ministry any who go for a hike on their Sabbath day? I prefer the revision which states that leaders are to be *"instructed by* the historic confessional standards of the church." Where previously it commanded "obedience to scripture," the revised version calls for "obedience to Jesus Christ, under the authority of Scripture."

I like some of the revisions. However, it is likely that the media will play only upon the change in wording regarding fidelity and chastity. The new wording calls for Presbyterian leaders to maintain "fidelity and integrity in marriage or singleness, and in all relationships of life." By broadening this area, many in the media will argue that the Presbyterian Church has undone what was voted through last year. While I have grave reservations about the direction this revised amendment could be interpreted, there is more to it than what the media tells us.

Before we believe what the media says about this topic or anything else, let us practice the discipline of study. We need to ask many questions in order to get to the truth. Let us recall that last year's media sensationalized this issue across the land. When a Presbytery voted in favor of Amendment B, it was reported as though Presbyterians were gay bashers. When another Presbytery voted against Amendment B, it was reported as though Presbyterians no longer believed that husbands and wives needed to be faithful in their marriages. Whichever way the vote went, the media skewed it to make it sensational.

While we can use this spiritual discipline in our study of science, relationships, media, and literature, it is most helpful in our understanding of the Bible. I appreciate how many of the men in our Saturday morning Bible study refer to commentaries to help them clarify their understanding of Scripture. While the commentaries of Barkley seem to be the most popular among our men, it is important to stretch our thinking by reading even the material with which we disagree.

A few weeks ago I began reading and reflecting on a new novel by Norman Mailer. *The Gospel According to the Son* is an interesting fictional piece which attempts to present the inner thoughts of Jesus. Pretending to write an account of Jesus' life as though it were dictated directly by Jesus, Norman Mailer has some interesting insights. I appreciate the way this novel emphasizes Jesus' humanity. On the other hand, I have some serious disagreements with several portions.

For instance, when Mailer recounts the story of Jesus' calming the wind and waves on the Sea of Galilee, he presents Jesus' thoughts as follows: "So I said to the wind, 'Be still.' And soon there was calm. I do not know if I can say that this miracle was mine. Even on awakening I could sense that the end of the storm was near."[1]

If Jesus could sense that the storm was almost over, why could his fishermen disciples not discern this? Why were these seasoned fishermen scared enough to wake Jesus up and ask for help if the storm was abating? If Jesus did not really perform a miracle, then why did he challenge his disciples with having too little faith? While I disagree with many such stories in this novel, I find it helpful in forcing me to ask questions which compel me to search the gospels for deeper insights.

In my last message we considered the importance of the discipline of meditation on the Scriptures. I used the example of my older son at about age four meditating on the story of Abraham's offering his son Isaac on the altar. My son had reversed the roles of father and son so that God was asking the son to offer his father on the altar. Meditation, we saw last time, is a way to get at the feelings in the Bible stories so that we can see ourselves in the text.

When we approach the Bible with the discipline of study, we study the background and history, analyzing the culture and writing styles of Bible stories. A study of this famous Bible story about Abraham's offering his son on the altar reveals that many ancient cultures surrounding Israel practiced child sacrifice. In pagan cultures it was not uncomon for a father to sacrifice his firstborn to his god. When we realize this, it helps us appreciate the fact that God was not asking anything from Abraham which was not required by the fertility religions of the Canaanites. What made Israel distinctive, however, was that God stopped Abraham from killing his son Isaac. A substitute animal was accepted in place of Isaac.

This idea of substitute sacrifice became central to the rest of the Bible. When the nation of Israel was set free from its bondage to Egypt, it was by each family substituting a lamb on the evening of the Passover. Every time Israel participated in the Passover meal, it was reminded that God allows substitute sacrifices in place of the firstborn.

This idea carried over into the New Testament. Our definition of salvation is that Jesus took our place as substitute. While we ought to be judged and punished for our sins, God offers Jesus as our substitute. When Jesus died on the cross, he took our place so that we could be forgiven. When we accept Jesus as our Lord and Savior, we are realizing that Jesus took our punishment, and now we are free to live gratefully since God loves us unconditionally.

The last day of Vacation Bible School I had the junior high class watch a portion of the movie *Jesus*. We read the crucifixion story from Luke's gospel and discussed why Jesus had died and rose from the dead. Some of the children had never heard that Jesus died for them. They had never realized that their sins could be forgiven by asking Jesus to be their substitute. It was wonderful to watch these youth ask one question after another as the implications of Jesus' life became clearer.

The discipline of study invites us to follow Jesus by asking questions. Therefore, let me question: Have you asked Jesus to be your substitute sacrifice? If not yet, why not now?

---

[1] Norman Mailer, *The Gospel According to the Son* (New York: Random House, 1997) 92-93.

The Discipline of
Solitude

For God alone my soul waits in silence;
  from him comes by salvation.
He only is my rock and my salvation,
  my fortress; I shall not be greatly moved.

Psalm 62:1-2

And after he had dismissed the crowds, he went up into the
hills by himself to pray.

Matthew 14:23

"We live in a noisy, busy world. *Silence* and *solitude* are not
twentieth-century words. They fit the era of Victorian lace,
high-buttoned shoes, and kerosene lamps better than our age of
television, video arcades, and joggers wired with earphones. We
have become a people with an aversion to quiet and an uneasiness
with being alone."[1]

While there are certainly exceptions to this general statement,
I agree with Jean Fleming's analysis of our culture in her book
Finding Focus in a Whirlwind World. I first realized how much I
avoided silence and solitude when we lived in an Indian village in
Alaska. I quickly learned that the Tlinget people were much more
comfortable with silence than I was. It took some time for me to
grow patient with silence in the midst of conversations with Tlinget
people.

While living in Alaska, I once heard a speaker describe
studies of language among different cultures. The person described

43

the fact that our middle-class American culture tends to expect quick answers to questions and will often interrupt silence to keep the conversation going. The speaker then reminded the crowd that most Native American cultures consider interruptions and hasty answers to be uncomfortable and even impolite. I had made this discovery on my own through my experiences of living among Native American people.

When I asked a question of a Tlinget, it was polite to let several seconds pass in silence while the person reflected and formulated a response. Short sentences combined with long pauses was normal conversational style for Tlinget people. I was used to interrupting and jumping in with half-baked thoughts from my middle-class background. The idea of carefully formulating a response before speaking was not part of my culture. Learning to communicate cross-culturally with these people involved my having to become comfortable with silence.

While I would not recommend that you view the movie *Fargo,* due to its R-rated violence, there was a humorous scene in the movie which reminded me of my early days among Tlinget people. One of the villains is driving a car with his co-conspirator in crime riding as the passenger. The passenger just sits and hardly ever says anything. The driver, uncomfortable with silence, tries in vain to keep the conversation going. Finally, in exasperation the driver says something like, "Fine! You want to just sit there and not talk? Well two can play that game. Let's just see how you like it if I stop talking to you! You won't like it one bit! I'm just going to stop talking and let you feel how it is to ride with someone who won't talk. O.K., then, I'm not going to say anything else. You won't like it when I treat you the same way. Let's just see how you like it! I'm going to stop talking and let you just sit in silence...." The problem is that the driver just can't stand to be quiet.

Many of us are uncomfortable with silence and solitude. For us to become more like Jesus, we must learn to practice the discipline of solitude. The discipline of solitude can be defined as *the act of voluntarily withdrawing from others in order to become quiet and be with God.*

Jesus set the example of solitude. Many times we read in the gospels that Jesus withdrew from the crowds in order to be alone. He knew how to balance his busy schedule with his need for quiet.

One of the main reasons Jesus practiced the discipline of solitude was to discern God's will. Jesus withdrew to quiet places in order to clarify his ministry to Galilee (Mark 1:35). He spent time in solitude before calling the first disciples (Luke 4:42). He spent time alone before naming the twelve apostles (Luke 6:12). Many of his miracles were often preceded by moments of solitude (Matthew 14:23).

How often do we wonder what God's will is for us and then fail to take the time for solitude in order to hear God's answer? Like a middle-class person living in the midst of Native Americans, we think we can ask God a question and receive an immediate response. I think God converses with us more like a Native American, with carefully chosen words in the midst of long pauses. If we are not in the habit of listening for this kind of communication, we may miss what God wants to tell us.

One of the great Christian missionaries of the nineteenth century was Hudson Taylor. He traveled to China to evangelize in Asia. In his early thirties, having served a few years in China, exhausted and in desperate need of renewal, he returned to his homeland to update his medical studies and recover. It was while Taylor was living back in England that he began to feel a tug at his heart to start a new mission program to China. All the missions to China at that time focussed on the coastal cities. He saw a need for a mission enterprise to take the gospel inland.

Hudson Taylor struggled for some time with this idea. His greatest fear was that he would become responsible for the fund-raising and missionary recruiting if he founded this new mission agency. He saw no way that he could do these demanding things. He was already struggling with his own deteriorating health and weariness: How could he possibly be used by God to start a whole new mission?

It was while seeking to recuperate at the beach home of friends that Hudson Taylor realized that he needed solitude more than anything else. He knew God had a call for him, but he had not been able to be alone long enough to really listen. On Sunday, June 25, 1865, Hudson Taylor left his friend's home and went for a walk along the sandy beach. He knew that it was time to make a decision as to whether or not to proceed with his vision for a new mission organization. In the quietness of the waves he listened for God. Suddenly the clear thought came to his mind. If God were calling him to found this new mission, the responsibility for the funding and recruiting was ultimately up to God. Taylor saw himself as God's servant who must leave both the responsibility and the results with God. His personal journal reflects that he slept well that night, and his wife noticed a significant change in his attitude from that day forward. Thus, Hudson Taylor founded the China Inland Mission which continues as the Overseas Missionary Fellowship today.[2]

While Jesus practiced the discipline of solitude primarily to know God's will, we also have another important reason to practice this discipline. We need to know ourselves. The sad truth is that we do not know ourselves well enough to serve God wholeheartedly. We shy away from being honest about our own shadow sides of our personalities. We sometimes think if we do not admit some problem in our lives, it will go away on its own. The discipline of solitude forces us to leave the distractions behind so we can discover who we really are.

King Philip of Macedonia, Alexander the Great's father, was once considering buying a horse named Bucephalus. However, when the attendants brought the horse to the field to test him, the horse was so unmanageable and vicious that King Philip decided not to pay the price for the finelooking animal. As the horse was being led away, the boy Alexander spoke up and offered to break the horse. The King challenged his son's arrogance in thinking that he could do what trained horsemen could not. When young Alexander claimed he could ride the horse, his father made a bet with him. If Alexander were not able to manage the horse, the king must pay the price of the animal. As the accompanying crowd listened and laughed at the royal father and son, the wager was settled. Young Alexander then ran to the horse and took hold of the bridle. Pulling the horse's face toward the sun, he mounted the horse and successfully rode him.

How could Alexander do what trained horsemen could not do? He had noticed something of which no one else seemed aware: Alexander had noticed that the horse was afraid of his own shadow. He realized that if he turned the horse toward the sun, the horse would no longer shy away from its own shadow and would become calm. Thus, Alexander used this insight to his advantage.[3]

Like Alexander's horse, we need to face the light. Instead of being afraid of the shadows of the failures and frailties of our personalities, we are invited by God in the discipline of solitude to be honest with ourselves. Such honesty can go deep when we turn off the distractions and draw intentionally close to God. In solitude we can discover our strengths and our weaknesses.

I am reading Billy Graham's autobiography *Just As I Am*. I am impressed by the genuine honesty of Dr. Graham's awareness of his own limitations. He tells about his confusion and struggles to discern God's will in his early evangelistic calling. He was serving as a college president, the youngest college president in that day, and also feeling called to the work of traveling evangelism. Billy Graham confesses that his travels had taken him away from his family to the extent that he saw his young daughter in the arms of a relative and asked, "Whose baby is this?"

The Los Angeles Crusade of 1949 was the watershed in Billy Graham's becoming a world famous evangelist. Just before that crusade Billy Graham took time out of his busy schedule to be alone with God. I think it was because of the discipline of solitude that Billy Graham became the evangelist he is today.

As he describes his own struggles, Dr. Billy Graham writes that Chuck Templeton, one of his best friends, had decided to pursue a scholarly career of Bible study. Templeton told Graham that today's Christian must keep up with the latest theology and scholarship. Templeton had recently completed his early studies at Princeton Seminary where he was learning to question many of the affirmations which Billy Graham believed. Templeton pointed out that the Bible was full of inconsistencies. He told Graham that Graham's preaching was out of date. Billy Graham's vocabulary was years behind the times, and his faith was too simple. Templeton warned that Billy Graham would be left in the dust if he did not adapt his theology to keep up with the times.

Simultaneously a Sunday school teacher named Henrietta Mears was meeting with Dr. Graham to encourage him to hold on to the old truths of the gospel. Billy Graham felt torn between the advice of his friend Chuck Templeton, who was becoming very intellectual, and this wise, older Sunday school teacher from Hollywood Presbyterian Church. Dr. Graham knew that he could not preach the upcoming series of evangelistic meetings in Los Angeles with a divided heart. He began by studying everything he could about issues of doubt. He read his Bible thoroughly in order to resolve his questions. However, after the discipline of study, he still had no certainty about God's will for his preaching. So he withdrew from others to be alone with God.

Billy Graham recalls that he walked out into the woods and set his Bible down on a stump. It was too dark to read the words of the Bible. He knelt at that stump and prayed, asking for God's will in his life. After struggling for a while in prayer, Billy Graham then did something for which I greatly respect him. He admitted his limited knowledge and his need to totally depend on God. He writes as follows:

> The exact wording of my prayer is beyond recall, but it must have echoed my thoughts: "O God! There are many things in this book I do not understand...."
>
> I was trying to be on the level with God, but something remained unspoken. At last the Holy Spirit freed me to say it. "Father, I am going to accept this as Thy Word—by *faith!* I'm going to allow faith to go beyond my intellectual questions and doubts, and I will believe this to be your inspired Word."[4]

Dr. Graham concludes this section of his life by describing his peace at feeling that a spiritual battle had been fought and won in his heart. The Los Angeles Crusade, which was planned to last for three weeks, lasted eight weeks. The crowds swelled from a few hundred to several thousand. Several prominent personalities experienced conversions at this crusade. It was during this crusade that Billy Graham became a national celebrity with feature articles in the Hearst newspapers.

What I particularly like about the examples of Billy Graham and Hudson Taylor is that they each involve a relatively small amount of time. While there are some people who can take entire days or weeks in solitude, most of us need help practicing this discipline in the midst of our busy schedules. It does not take forty days of fasting and prayer to hear God; it frequently takes only a few minutes of solitude.

When was the last time we turned off the television and simply sat in silence for a few minutes? Do we really need to have the radio or stereo on around the house all day? If our days are too busy with commitments and interruptions, we may take time when we first wake in the morning to just be still and intentionally be with God for a moment. I know there are young mothers who can't even go to the bathroom without a child or husband in the vicinity. Susanna Wesley, mother of John and Charles and several other children, would sometimes feel overwhelmed with the noises of an active family of young children. At these times Susanna Wesley used to take her apron and pull it over her head for a moment of personal calm in the midst of the goings-on in the room at the time. The children were instructed that when Mommy pulled the apron over her face, she was not to be interrupted. The older children were instructed to take care of the younger ones for a few moments until Mom was ready to deal with the family again.[5]

The irony of the spiritual discipline of solitude is that it is probably the easiest and the hardest at the same time. It is easy to practice, but it is hard to make into a regular habit. Solitude will not happen by itself. If we do not make the time in our schedules, we will never learn this discipline. Yet the discipline of solitude can bring us so much closer to God that it is worth the effort. When will you take a few moments with God this week?

---

[1] Jean Fleming, *Finding Focus in a Whirlwind World* (Dallas: Roper Press, 1991) 73.

[2] Donald S. Whitney, *Spiritual Disciplines for the Christian Life* (Colorado Springs: NavPress, 1991) 183-184.

³ Plutarch, "The Lives of the Noble Grecians and Romans," *Great Books of the Western World,* vol. 14 (Chicago: Encyclopedia Britannica, Inc., 1952) 353.

⁴ Billy Graham, *Just As I Am* (San Francisco: Harper/Zondervan, 1997) 139.

⁵ Donald S. Whitney, *Spiritual Disciplines for the Christian Life,* 190.

The Discipline of Service

He who is kind to the poor lends to the Lord,
and he will repay him for his deed.

Proverbs 19:17

"When the Son of Man comes in his glory, and all the angels with him, then he will sit on the throne of his glory. All the nations will be gathered before him, and he will separate people one from another as a shepherd separates the sheep from the goats, and he will put the sheep at his right hand and the goats at the left. Then the king will say to those at his right hand, 'Come, you that are blessed by my Father, inherit the kingdom prepared for you from the foundation of the world; for I was hungry and you gave me food, I was thirsty and you gave me something to drink, I was a stranger and you welcomed me, I was naked and you gave me clothing, I was sick and you took care of me, I was in prison and you visited me.' Then the righteous will answer him, 'Lord, when was it that we saw you hungry and gave you food, or thirsty and gave you something to drink? And when was it that we saw you a stranger and welcomed you, or naked and gave you clothing? And when was it that we saw you sick or in prison and visited you?' And the king will answer them, 'Truly I tell you, just as you did it to one of the least of these who are members of my family, you did it to me.' Then he will say to those at his left hand, 'You that are accursed, depart from me into the eternal fire prepared for the devil and his angels;

for I was hungry and you gave me no food, I was thirsty and you gave me nothing to drink, I was a stranger and you did not welcome me, naked and you did not give me clothing, sick and in prison and you did not visit me.' Then they also will anser, 'Lord, when was it that we saw you hungry or thirsty or a stranger or naked or sick or in prison, and did not take care of you?' Then he will answer them, 'Truly I tell you, just as you did not do it to one of the least of these, you did not do it to me.' And these will go away into eternal punishment, but the righteous into eternal life."

Matthew 25:31-46 NRSV

"WANTED: Young, skinny, wiry fellows not over eighteen. Must be expert riders willing to risk daily. Orphans preferred." This was the recruiting ad which ran in 1860 in a San Francisco paper. The young men recruited were to serve as riders for the Pony Express. With the words about daily risks, this ad must have fired the imaginations of many young men because the Pony Express was never short on riders. With excitement and wonder young men signed up to ride a horse for seventy-five to one hundred miles a day, trading horses every fifteen to twenty-five miles. They were allowed to carry minimal supplies which included the bag of mail, some bacon, flour, cornmeal, and a small medical pack. To increase speed and mobility, the riders wore short-sleeve shirts even through the snowy winter months. What an exciting life!

The reality, however, was much more mundane. Long hours, loneliness, and boredom were the main experiences for most of the riders. As adventuresome as it sounded on paper, the reality was that this job, like most jobs, primarily involved mundane things. Riding a horse at breakneck speed for hours on end can become as tiring and unfulfilling as anything else. In fact, the Pony Express only lasted seventeen months, from April 1860 to November 1861. It was replaced by the telegraph.[1]

Like the young men who thought their lives would be glorious and exciting if they signed up to ride for the Pony Express, some people think that becoming a Christian and serving God is some glorious and exciting experience. The truth is that serving God mostly comes down to the ordinary, mundane details of life. While there may be moments of extreme satisfaction and thrill when something dynamic happens and some prayer is miraculously answered, most of us live our Christian faith by remaining faithful in the daily routines.

Dr. Fred Craddock is one of my favorite preachers. He tells about his feelings when he attended the junior high camp sponsored by his denomination. On the last night of camp the youth would sit around the campfire as the director challenged them to give their lives to Christ. Dr. Craddock recalls thinking that the invitation to give one's life to Christ was really an invitation to something dramatic and glorious. His youthful mind pictured himself as a missionary to some headhunting, tribal people. He would serve in some distant, exotic place and then complete his ministry by having the pagan cannibals kill him. After his death the entire tribe would feel so bad about murdering a faithful man of God that they would convert to Christianity. Then, the church would be built, and next to the church would be a memorial with his name on it. In the future, Christian families would come to this Christian village to view the memorial stone and tell the story of how Fred Craddock gave his life for Jesus.

Dr. Craddock, having spun this wonderful fantasy of how he thought it was going to be if he gave his life to Christ, would then describe the reality of his years in Christian ministry. Most of ministry is unexciting. Like any other job, there are long periods of the boring maintenance of daily tasks punctuated by a few moments of exciting, miraculous happenings. He concluded this example from his own life with the comment that he assumed we gave our lives to Christ like signing a $1,000 check to the Lord. Now, as a mature Christian, he realizes that investing our lives for God involves spending a little bit of change each day. We invest our lives by being faithful with our dimes and nickels.

My experiences resonate with Dr. Craddock's description of the Christian life. When I moved to a mission church in an Alaskan village, I envisioned my life as a glorious adventure of living in another culture. I wanted to help bring these people to Christ through some great preaching. I pictured myself as being the greatest preacher the village had ever had. The reality was far different.

Soon after arriving, the oil heater in the church began to have problems. Many Saturday nights and Sunday mornings I spent on my knees trying to get the heater in the church basement to warm the sanctuary enough to hold services. Seminary had not prepared me to work on the heater and neither had growing up in Tucson. I knew nothing about how an oil heater worked. I would crawl around with a wrench in my hand and a prayer on my lips. Frequently the problems in the heater were beyond my limited abilities so that I needed to call one or two of the elders to come help me fix the heater. Occasionally we held a winter service without any heat. I recall watching the entire congregation (about twenty-five in attendance) sing hymns with wisps of condensation puffing from their mouths as they sang.

The second year in that church we had a toilet break in the basement. The leak was minor at first, but within a few days it was starting to cause a problem as water began to seep out of the bathroom and puddle on the floor in the hallway. I ordered the parts needed to fix the toilet. When they arrived, I learned that there was no main shut-off valve for our church's water system. I had to replace the broken toilet parts with the water spraying at full pressure. By the time I had the new parts in place, the entire basement had about four inches of standing water. The cleanup was frustrating.

This morning we are thinking about the spiritual discipline of service. It sounds exciting at first. We are called by God to share the work of bringing the kingdom of God on earth. We are invited by Christ to share in the drama of changing lives. The reality, however, is that this is the most humbling of spiritual disciplines. It generally involves doing the unappreciated, behind-the-scenes, yet necessary activities.

The little girl was heartbroken over the death of her kitten. As the mother tried to comfort her daughter, the mother said, "Just think, honey, Fluffy is in heaven with God." The child thought about this for a moment and then asked, "What would God want with a dead cat?"[2]

The Apostle James wrote a similar question, "What good is dead faith?" Since faith without works is dead, what good is it to claim to have faith without having any active way of showing faith? As someone has said, "Some people are so heavenly minded that they are no earthly good." The discipline of service forces our faith to be alive by putting our beliefs into action. As Jesus taught us, when we do a good deed for another, we are really doing it for Jesus himself.

Years ago I heard a presentation by a doctoral candidate whose research thesis revolved around the idea of Christian compassion. This graduate student had decided to study what there was in common among the Christians who risked their lives in Germany during World War II. His hypothesis was that the Christians who had been willing to risk arrest by helping the Jews to hide during the Nazi persecutions might have something in common. Indeed, after interviewing significant numbers of such Christians, he came to some interesting conclusions. First, he concluded that acts of compassionate service involved two important steps: The person seeking to help must be able to identify the need and then must be able to find a creative way to meet that need. He was struck in particular with how these Christians had an amazing ability to read other's body language and identify when someone needed help. He was told consistently that these people would walk into a crowded public area and be able to spot someone who needed help.

The second conclusion was what I found particularly intriguing. This graduate student was struck by the fact that almost all of the Christians who had distinguished themselves by helping the Jews escape from the Nazi persecutions had memorized Matthew 25 as children. "Lord, when did we see you hungry and feed you?" "Lord, when did we see you thirsty and give you a drink?" "Lord, when did we clothe you or visit you in prison?" "When you did it for the least of these, my brothers, you did it to me."

How do we avoid having a useless, dead faith? The same way the Sea of Galilee avoids becoming like the Dead Sea. The Dead Sea is a collection of chemicals so heavy that the human body cannot dive under water. People lie on top of the water in the Dead Sea. The sulfur smells that bubble up from the Dead Sea are disgusting. It is called the Dead Sea because it hosts no living plants or animals. In contrast, the Sea of Galilee is full of life. The Sea of Galilee, just a few miles north of the Dead Sea, abounds with plants and fish. What is the difference?

The same river flows into both lakes. Yet the northern Sea of Galilee is alive while the southern Dead Sea is dead. The difference is that the northern Sea of Galilee is both a recipient and a donor. The river flows in from the north, replenishing the oxygen and bringing a supply of healthy nutrients. Then, at the southern end of the Sea of Galilee the Jordan River empties to continue its travels south. The Sea of Galilee has a constant change of water as the river enters and exits on opposite ends of the lake. The Dead Sea receives this same source of water; however, it is so low that there is no continuation of the river. Thus, the Dead Sea only receives, but never gives. As the water evaporates and the chemicals are left behind, this lowest point on earth becomes the Dead Sea.

The discipline of service reminds us that we must give as well as receive if we are to be healthy, godly people. God has created every Christian to serve. The price of not serving is that our spirits slowly die. There is nobody too high to need this discipline.

We frequently refer to the Apostle Thomas as Doubting Thomas. This is the disciple who said he would not believe unless he actually touched the nail prints in Jesus' hands. After challenging the resurrection stories, Thomas became a devoted follower of Christ. While the Bible does not tell us any more about this apostle, there are traditions in early church history that say Thomas became the apostle to evangelize India. According to a long standing tradition, Thomas arrived in India and was questioned by a King Gundafor as to his profession. Thomas described himself as one who had been an apprentice to a carpenter. Thomas further explained that he could build palaces worthy of a king. King Gundafor hired Thomas to build him a magnificent palace. A great deal of money was paid, and the king left on an extended vacation.

When the king returned to his home in India, he found no palace waiting for him. He called Thomas before him and questioned him as to why the new palace had not been built. Thomas explained that he had given the money to the poor and needy so that this king could have a palace in the kingdom of heaven. The unhappy king was extremely angry to learn that his money had been wasted on the poor. Thomas was arrested and kept in prison. While Thomas was awaiting execution, the king's brother died. Some days later the king had a vision of the brother's describing the magnificent palace which was waiting for the king due to Thomas's faithful investment of the funds in God's work. The king awoke from the dream and released Thomas. According to the end of this traditional story, King Gundafor was then baptized and became a devout Christian.[3]

President Lincoln was in the habit of visiting hospitals where his wounded Union soldiers were being treated. One day the President approached the bedside of a young soldier who was close to death. President Lincoln asked the soldier if there were something he could do for him. The soldier asked if he would write a letter home to his mother. The soldier dictated as the President wrote, "My dearest mother, I was badly hurt while doing my duty. I'm afraid I'm not going to recover. Don't grieve too much for me, please. Kiss Mary and John for me. May God bless you and Father." The weakened soldier was unable to continue, so the President signed the boy's name and added his own words. "Written for your son by Abraham Lincoln." The boy asked to see the note and when he had read it asked, "Are you really the President?" Lincoln assured him he was and asked if there were anything else he needed. The boy asked to hold the President's hand. The President remained at the bedside until the boy died.[4]

The discipline of service is not just needed for kings and presidents; it is an important spiritual discipline for all of us. A few months ago we hosted the memorial service for former church member Dee Riggs. She is remembered in our community for her countless hours of public service and her many acts of genuine Christian charity. She helped found several organizations which continue serving in the name of Christ, including the local Habitat for Humanity. At her memorial service I told some of her stories which were written in a biography about her life. When Dee was entering college, she developed a serious medical condition which required surgery. After she had recovered, she went to negotiate a payment schedule to pay the doctor's bill. The doctor forgave the entire fee and simply told Dee to spend the rest of her life looking for others less fortunate and then do something for them. Later in her college years she served the local campus chapel by playing the piano. She told me that she once heard the Reverend Harry Emerson Fosdick guest preach in the college chapel. At the close of the service this famous radio preacher approached Dee and told her one sentence that changed her perspective and her life. He said, "Happiness is the by-product of a meaningful life of service." When Dee told me that story, I could sense some emotions in her voice. She then said, "Bruce, teach the young people of the next generation that happiness is not an end in itself. It is the by-product of a meaningful life of service."

Dee Riggs had discovered what each of us must learn: We cannot have a living faith unless we practice the discipline of service. This spiritual discipline is one which presidents as well as ordinary citizens must practice. Kings and apostles, pastors and doctors, mothers and children, we are all invited to follow Jesus by serving our neighbors.

For me the most difficult aspect of this humbling spiritual discipline is that we see such slow progress and so little effect for our actions. If we are to learn to practice this discipline with a sense of joy, we must learn to recognize and celebrate minute results. The Kingdom of God comes in tiny, seemingly insignificant steps.

Merl was in high school when we first met him. He came to our home to visit during the second year of our ministry in Hoonah. He learned that we had a computer game on our television and asked if he could play the game. For an hour or more he would sit and play the game. Kathy would offer him something to drink, but he seldom accepted the offer. In fact, he barely conversed with us. Merl's vocabulary seemed to consist more of grunts and nods than real words strung together in sentences.

Near the end of that school year I invited Merl to come to summer camp with me. I was directing a high school camp and thought he could use some positive influence in his life. By that time I had learned that his parents were alcoholics. He had been abused at home and learned to stay away when his parents were drinking. He wanted to go to camp but had no way to pay the fees. I asked our church elders if we could provide a scholarship. Merl was given the scholarship. After the camp was over, he began to help me clean up around the church. Several Saturdays, when I had some small chore or task, Merl would be at my side helping. In the afternoons he continued to drop by our house to play the video games. I recall the day Kathy greeted me at the door with the exciting news that Merl had said two words in a row: Thank you. He thanked Kathy as he was leaving!

Over that school year we encouraged Merl as he decided to compete in school sports. He chose to wrestle and made the varsity team. In fact, by the spring semester we discovered that Merl had earned a varsity letter. Even though he had a part-time job at school, his parents took all his money, so he had no way to buy himself a varsity letter jacket. Our church took up a special offering without his knowledge and ordered a letter jacket for him. Merl was so surprised the night of the awards presentation when he was given the jacket.

By the time we moved from the village, Merl was starting to string together phrases of five or six words. Sometimes he opened up and talked with me in complete sentences. He talked only when nobody else was around.

The last time Kathy and I saw him was when we were living in Sitka, and Merl had come to town for some sports competition. He walked up to me and smiled. He was wearing his letter jacket. He started the conversation and talked for several minutes. He again thanked us for being his friends.

The discipline of service may seem like an unrewarding spiritual discipline until we get used to looking for the minute, little steps people are making toward God. When we notice the little changes, it becomes wonderful to realize that something we did that may seem small and insignificant can be bringing real change to another's life.

A man was looking to visit a church and wandered into an old-fashioned Quaker meeting. The meeting of Quakers involved sitting in silence as each person entered into the spiritual disciplines of prayer and meditation. The visitor sat for several minutes in the silence and then finally leaned over to someone near and asked, "When does the service begin?" The Quaker whispered back, "The service begins when the worship ends."

---

[1] Donald S. Whitney, *Spiritual Disciplines for the Christian Life* (Colorado Springs: NavPress, 1991) 109-110.

[2] Bob Phillips, *The World's Greatest Collection of Heavenly Humor* (Eugene: Harvest House Publishers, 1982) 56.

[3] Michael Walsh, *Butler's Lives of the Saints* (San Fransisco: HarperCollines, 1991) 203-204.

[4] Jack Canfield and Mark Victor Hansen, *A 3rd Serving of Chicken Soup for the Soul* (Deerfield Beach: Health Communications, Inc., 1996) 49-50.

The Discipline of Submission

Be subject to one another out of reverence for Christ.
Ephesians 5:21

A dispute also arose among them, which of them was to be regarded as the greatest. And he said to them, "The kings of the Gentiles exercise lordship over them; and those in authority over them are called benefactors. But not so with you; rather let the greatest among you become as the youngest, and the leader as one who serves. For which is the greater, one who sits at table, or one who serves? Is it not the one who sits at table? But I am among you as one who serves."
Luke 22:24-27

Last Sunday evening's service was special. Our church hosted a youth group which had come to Arizona from Minnesota to do a work project on the Navajo Reservation. All twenty-seven of the youth were at the evening service along with their adult advisors. Since this youth group had not heard any of my previous sermons on this summer's theme of disciplines, I asked if any of the youth had seen or heard of the new wrist bracelets with the letters WWJD. To my astonishment they all held up their arms and revealed that the entire youth group was wearing these Christian bracelets. They had put them on their arms in a commissioning service at the airport just two days before.

In recent weeks I have received newspaper clippings from church members with relatives in South Dakota and Oklahoma about the increasing popularity of these bracelets. With more and more people wearing them, it is exciting to see that these bracelets are sweeping our nation. It was moving when one of our church members asked one of the youth about his bracelet and then seeing the young man take off his bracelet and put it on her arm as his gift. He explained that the group wanted to give these bracelets to anyone who asked about them. Perhaps these bracelets could be an answer to our prayers for God to send a wave of revival and renewal across our country.

Some of our own people in the evening service had missed the two sermons that kicked off this summer's series of sermons and had no idea what I was talking about regarding these bracelets with the letters WWJD. It reminded me that perhaps it is time to review the meaning of these letters as well as the central theme of these sermons on the spiritual disciplines. For those who do not know, the initials WWJD stand for the question, "What would Jesus do?" This was the question which a pastor asked his congregation in the classic, best-selling novel *In His Steps* by Charles Sheldon. We learned several weeks ago that this novel was the best-selling novel in America for sixty years, from its publication in 1897 until the mid-1950's. I began this summer series of sermons by challenging our congregation to include this book in their summer reading. I am pleased that several have reported to me that they are enjoying reading *In His Steps*.

When we ask the question, "What would Jesus do?" and then truly seek to be faithful to what Jesus would do, we become the people God wants us to be. The key is that we not only ask the question, but genuinely try to follow wherever it may take us. We are discovering this summer that being like Jesus is costly.

Two brothers, ages five and three, were arguing over who would get the first pancakes one Saturday morning. As their mother prepared the breakfast, she became tired of their arguing and decided to use it as a chance to reinforce a moral lesson. "If Jesus were sitting here, he would say, 'Let my brother have the first pancake. I can wait,'" she explained. The older brother immediately turned to his younger brother and said, "Okay, Ryan, *you* be Jesus!"[1]

Of course, the purpose of asking, "What would Jesus do?" is so that we can be more like Jesus rather than expect others to be Jesus to us. After introducing this question to guide our moral and ethical choices, I reminded our congregation that the only way we can find the answer to this question is to commit ourselves to practicing the spiritual disciplines which Jesus practiced. Thus, we have been considering a different spiritual discipline each week over this summer. Last week we looked at the discipline of service: The next logical discipline is today's spiritual discipline of submission.

Submission is perhaps the most unpopular and difficult spiritual discipline. Perhaps part of the difficulty with this spiritual discipline is that people mistakenly think submission means acting the part of a carpet and letting people walk all over us. This is *not* what we mean by the submission. The spiritual discipline of submission requires a high degree of positive self-esteem and healthy self-awareness. We can submit and deny ourselves only when we are aware that God loves us totally. Jesus was confident enough in his calling and purpose to practice this discipline by washing the disciples' feet at the Last Supper. If he had felt insecure about his value to God, Jesus could never have taken the towel and washed their feet in this act of submission.

Not only is this spiritual discipline difficult because it is misunderstood, it also is easily abused. Under a twisted form of this discipline we have seen people in Heaven's Gate and Jonestown commit mass suicide. Something is wrong and dangerous when the discipline of submission becomes a way for manipulative leaders to keep their followers in absolute obedience.

Consider a common misinterpretation of submission. One of the most misquoted passage of the Bible in recent years is Ephesians 5:22: "Wives, submit yourselves to your husbands." When I think of how this verse has been misinterpreted, I recall the first time I ever encouraged a wife to divorce her abusive, unfaithful husband. Dolly was a college student on our campus in Sitka, Alaska. She had come to me for a few months with grave concerns

63

about her marriage. Her husband only verbally abused her without actually raising his fist. When she had talked to her pastor about her problems the pastor had told her to remain with the husband as long as he did not actually hit her. She came to me for a second opinion. I listened to her description of his manipulations and use of fear over her. I listened to her suspicions that he was having an affair since he frequently sneaked out at night and returned in the early hours of the morning. She told me about his problem with alcohol. She had put up with these problems for a few years and now was wondering if she were doomed by God to live a life of quiet desperation. Was this God's will? Should she resign herself to a life of unhappiness with an uncaring husband? Must she lie awake at night and worry that this man might sexually abuse her older daughter, born from a previous marriage?

Having listened to Dolly's fears and learned more about the personality of her spouse, I asked her husband if he would come in with her for counseling. He refused. He was angry at the very idea that his wife thought they needed marriage counseling when he considered their marriage to be doing fine. Finally, she made the decision to leave him. I agreed to help her move out, so she could take the children with her to a home for battered women. I witnessed her husband's manipulative style the day I helped her pack her things and move out. I recall her husband's rage-filled threats that she would go to hell for breaking apart their family. I listened as he switched to tears and promises that he would never drink again. I watched him try to hold her down as he shouted at her. Then, I listened as he gave her his version of this passage from the Bible: "Wife, submit to your husband!"

In order to avoid this serious misinterpretation of the Scriptures, we must take a moment to review the original Greek text. Would it surprise you to find out that the verb *submit* does not appear in this verse regarding wives? In fact, there is no verb at all in this verse. The actual Greek text simply says, "Wives to your husbands." We must add the verb by extrapolating from the immediate context. Since the previous verse says, "Submit yourselves to one another out of reverence for Christ," it makes sense to draw the verb *submit* from this verse into the next verse.

Thus, by implication we have the translation, "Wives submit to your husbands." If we are translating by implication, we ought to be faithful to the entire passage by also reading the next obvious implication, "Husbands submit to your wives." If the thought is that we are to submit to one another out of reverence for Christ, then submission goes both directions: wives to husbands and husbands to wives.

I suspect the reason this passage is so often misinterpreted is that most of us have a problem with the whole idea of submission. We live in a culture which admires individualism and celebrates independence. We are a people who do not want to have to submit to others since we want to protect our own rights. The spiritual discipline of submission flies in the face of much of what our culture teaches us. It is at this point that our society is probably the most unchristian.

Let us consider this unpopular spiritual discipline of submission. We can define it as the willingness to give up our rights in order to let God be God. When we practice this discipline, we dare to believe that God can work through the decisions of others. The benefit of this spiritual discipline is that we stop having to argue our own viewpoint. We can release our hurts and let God deal with the situation. The spiritual discipline of submission allows us to be free from having to be right. Most of us do not realize that having to be right is a terrible burden which weighs us down and keeps us from enjoying God's rule in our lives.

A woman was tired of having her husband go hunting every fall without her, so she asked if she could go hunting with him. She prepared by taking gun-safety classes as well as target practice. She became comfortable enough with the rifle so that she was ready for the big weekend.

Early on the first morning of the hunt, the husband and wife agreed to split up and go around opposite sides of a small hill. If there were deer in the area, the husband thought that either he or his wife might get a good shot as one of them startled the deer into the open. About an hour into the hunt the husband heard a rifle shot and then a second shot. He waited to see if any deer might be scared toward him. When he was sure there were no deer, he walked toward the sound of the two shots. As he came through the woods, he heard his wife arguing with a man. "I shot it first! This is my deer!" The man was sputtering in anger. Just as the husband arrived, he heard the man say, "All right, lady, its your deer. Just let me take my saddle off of it!"

Just as this woman argued over the deer, so many of us have a sinful tendency to argue as though we are the only ones who are right, and everyone else is wrong. We take minor issues and let them get all out of proportion as we bicker over fine points. Of course, this is not new to Christianity. Jesus' disciples argued with each other about who was the most important to Jesus. Jesus reminded them that the best disciple is the one who is most willing to give up his rights and simply serve others. Jesus turned the image of greatness around by reminding the disciples that he had acted as a servant rather than demanding his rights to be served. Jesus knelt at their feet and washed their feet and then tried to instruct the disciples about greatness in God's kingdom. True greatness before God involves the ability to sacrifice our own rights in order to love others.

When I was young and naive, I used to know everything there was to know about rearing children. I would watch others battle with their teenagers and silently say to myself, "I'll never do that!" Now that our own four children are teenagers and young adults, I readily admit that I know almost nothing about rearing children. When our children were young, I used to tell myself, "I will never say to my children, 'Because I said so!'" I used to despise the phrase, "Because I'm your dad, that's why!"

However, I have learned that children do not have the maturity to practice the spiritual discipline of submission. Frequently the issue is not that we as parents have not expressed ourselves clearly, reasonably, and definitively. The issue is that the youth simply does not agree with our reasons and refuses to submit. They are not asking with a whiny voice, "Why?" because they did not hear or understand us. We are tempted to ask sarcastically, "What part of *No* don't you understand?" They heard and understood. They simply do not like the answer and do not want to submit to the parents' authority.

I appreciate the way that many Native American tribes teach their youth to practice the discipline of submission. In many of the Plains Indian tribes there is a ritual of puberty called the Spirit Quest. This involves leaving the rest of the tribe in order to participate in extended periods of fasting and meditation. During the abstinence from food and water, often combined with painful rituals which drain the youth's energy, the young man has a vision. Often the vision involves a spiritual guide and specific instructions for living a faithful life. Frequently the youth returns to the tribe with a special bundle of holy items which symbolize the spiritual power he has gained.

What I find very interesting is the way that the Sioux then take the youth through the process of initiation into adulthood. The youth returns with the description of his vision and tells it to the wise village elders. These holy men then help the youth construct his memory of the vision into a socially established norm for spiritual beliefs. Until the young man can retell his visionary story in a way that is acceptable to the village elders, his experience is not complete.[2]

This last week our older daughter traveled to Mexico with an Assembly of God youth group. They had prepared and raised funds for the week-long trip. The group performed Christian dramas in several Mexican towns. Ashley enjoyed her time with this youth group. I was particularly impressed with her attitude when she learned that all the girls on the trip were to wear extremely modest clothing. When she learned of the dress code for the trip, she discovered that she did not have a single dress that met the code. The dresses were to be full-length and could not cling to the body. The swimsuits had to be one-piece and extremely modest. Ashley had to buy a new wardrobe in order to go on the trip!

A year ago I could have heard Ashley argue with the youth director over such clothing codes. I would not have been surprised if she had refused to participate in the name of personal rights. After all, she has the right to wear whatever she chooses. Yet she realized that if she wanted to participate, she must abide by their youth group rules. Rather than argue, she chose to submit and participate in something that would nourish her faith. She is learning at sixteen that God desires us to practice the discipline of submission.

I can understand when children and youth have problems with this spiritual discipline. I know that it is common for young people to want to defend their rights and assert their independence and individuality. What I find astonishing is that some people who have walked with the Lord for fifty years or more have failed to learn this discipline. Many adults have never outgrown the immaturity of having to argue their rights. Let's face it: The discipline of submission requires a great deal maturity. To abide by someone else's decision, when we think they are wrong, is difficult if we think we must be right. To abide by someone else's decision, when we strongly disagree with their views, is not easy. We can only do it if we have a radical sense that God is in control and will work out matters for God's own glory.

Churches and denominations with unhealthy conflict are generally self-destructing because people do not spend enough time in prayer asking God to work his will. Instead, they take it on themselves to work the system to get their own desired ends. Some years ago I served on a synod committee which was forced every year to review one particular policy. Each year that I served, we voted the same way. Yet each year the policy was included on the agenda for debate. The first couple of years I simply listened and occasionally participated in the discussion. By the third or fourth time the issue had come to the committee, I began to wonder why we needed to keep discussing it over and over. I learned that one of the staff members of the synod did not agree with our previous decisions, so he was constantly asking the committee to reconsider our actions. The simple truth is that he refused to submit to the decision of God's people with whom he had committed himself.

How often have we seen this kind of thing happen? God's people in a church or denomination make a decision and those who are part of the group in disagreement refuse to submit. Rather than pray and believe that God is working, they play political games to get the outcome they desire. This is not the way our Lord intended the church to function.

Dan Hurlbert, a fellow pastor, recalls that everyone in his home church called her Grandma Moore. She was, according to his youthful categories, old. She was probably in her seventies when he first became aware of how active she was in their church. Grandma Moore continued to help with the church's youth group. She was always at the church potlucks. She was a pillar of the local church. When it came to a church debate, Grandma Moore was to be reckoned with.

Dan told me recently about the year that the local church held its war over the dishwasher. It might have been during the late sixties, and Dan was more of an observer than a player in the skirmishes and battles surrounding the dishwasher. Some women of the church decided that their growing church ought to have a commercial-size dishwasher to help with the cleanup after church, potluck meals. The younger women in particular felt that their time could be better used with their children than in cleaning and drying dishes. Grandma Moore was against it from the get-go.

When the issue finally came to an official congregational meeting, Grandma Moore expressed her views with passion. She reminded her fellow church members that she had been in that old kitchen for years. She was among the first to show up before a congregational meal and among the last to leave. She also told the rest of the people that she would lose valuable fellowship time with other women if they did not do the dishes together. Grandma Moore was a widow, and her time in the kitchen was that of valuable fellowship. She actually enjoyed doing the dishes as part of her service to the Lord and to her church. Finally, she reminded the congregation that the money could be better spent on other more worthy causes such as youth events and missions work. The debate continued for some time, but finally the vote was called.

When the votes were counted, Grandma Moore lost. Then, Dan recalls what happened next. Grandma Moore stood and asked for the privilege of the floor. When she was recognized, she slowly pulled out her checkbook from her purse and proceeded to write the first check for the new dishwasher fund.

The discipline of submission reminds us that the issues about which we worry and let ourselves get upset are often not as important as we thought. We do not have to be right or work the political system to get our own way when we practice this spiritual discipline. This spiritual discipline forces us to believe that God is working through our prayers and our genuine love for those with whom we disagree. As tough as this discipline is, we can be set free from our power games and bitterness when we accept this simple truth: God is God and we are not!

---

[1]Patti Greenberg Wollman and Merril Feinstein-Feit, "Wee Words of Wisdom," *McCalls* August 1997: 108.

[2]Sam D. Gill, *Native American Religions* (Belmont: Wadsworth Publishing Co., 1982) 100.

The Discipline of Confession

Are any among you suffering? They should pray. Are any among you cheerful? They should sing songs of praise. Are any among you sick? They should call for the elders of the church and have them pray over them, anointing them with oil in the name of the Lord. The prayer of faith will save the sick, and the Lord will raise them up; and anyone who has committed sins will be forgiven. Therefore confess your sins to one another, and pray for one another, so that you may be healed. The prayer of the righteous is powerful and effective.

James 5:13-16 NRSV

For by the grace given to me I say to everyone among you not to think of yourself more highly than you ought to think, but to think with sober judgment, each according to the measure of faith that God has assigned.

Romans 12:3 NRSV

Last week I attended a conference for clergy. Spending time in discussions with fellow pastors reminded me of the story of the three ministers who decided they needed to confess their secret sins to each other. The first pastor confessed that he had a drinking problem. Secretly he was drinking himself into a stupor each night. He had tried to stop but found himself powerless to change. The second pastor confessed that he had a gambling problem. He regularly drove to a distant casino and gambled his money away.

71

The third pastor listened intently to the first two confess, but then when they turned to him, he was extremely hesitant to be totally honest and share his character flaw. "I just can't tell you my major sin. You would both be horrified." The other two reminded him that confession was good for the soul. He argued that they would find it hard to listen to his confession, but they persisted in asking him to admit his worst sin. Finally, he admitted, "I have trouble maintaining confidentiality. I tend to spread rumors by telling others what I learn in secret. And I can't wait to get out of this room!"

Many of us think of confession as a Roman Catholic act where a faithful church member secretly confesses to a priest. Others of us associate the idea of confession with Pentecostalism and revivalism where people come forward and announce their horrible sins to the entire congregation. I heard about one man's confession at a revival meeting where he announced to the crowded tent meeting, "I've cheated and lied. I've beat my wife and gotten drunk. But one thing I never did: I never lost my religion!"

Most of us associate confession with feeling sorry for our sins. This is a misunderstanding of the spiritual discipline of confession. While this is one important aspect of confession, it is not all there is. If this were the only kind of confession, Jesus would never have needed to participate in this spiritual discipline since he never sinned. The Bible reminds us that Jesus was perfect, being without sin (2 Corinthians 5:21, 1 Peter 2:22). In fact, Jesus was unique in the fact that he was both God and human at the same time. Thus, if confession were only about our sins, it would never have been needed by Jesus.

In order to understand the spiritual discipline of confession, we need to define it as more than simply feeling sorry for our sins. In fact, we need to see confession as having little to do with our feelings at all. Confession is less about feelings and more about honesty. The spiritual discipline of confession could be defined as getting truly honest with God. When we admit the truth to ourselves, to God, and to others, no matter what the consequences, we are participating in the spiritual discipline of confession.

Jesus exemplified this spiritual discipline when he stood on trial before the court of elders. When they questioned him on religious doctrine and specifically asked if he were the Son of God, which in the Jewish language means that he was equating himself with God, Jesus made his truthful confession, "You are right in saying I am" (Luke 22:70). When Jesus was taken to Pilate's court and questioned on his political views, Pilate specifically asked Jesus, "Are you the king of the Jews?" Jesus' answer was an example of the spiritual discipline of confession when he replied, "Yes, it is as you say" (Luke 23:3).

The spiritual discipline of confession involves admitting the truth about both the shadow side and gifted side of ourselves. In some ways we are like God, because we have God-given strengths which make up our gifted side. In some ways we are far from God's will because we let our own sinfulness distract us from being all God wants us to be. This is our shadow side. In the discipline of confession we learn to be honest about both sides of ourselves. With Jesus we can confess that we are valued by God and gifted by God. We also can confess to sinfulness which Jesus never needed to confess. In other words, the spiritual discipline of confession helps us do what the Apostle Paul wrote to the Christians in Rome, "Do not think of yourself more highly than you ought, but rather think of yourself with sober judgment" (Romans 12:3).

A week ago I participated in a week-long, clergy seminar which included an activity titled "Shadow Work." The exercise took about two hours one afternoon. The preliminary activity took place just before lunch. We were asked to identify someone toward whom we felt a high degree of hostility. As we reflected on our hostile feelings, we were to examine our thoughts and consider whether there were some aspect of the other person's character which we despised. Once we had identified that which we despised about the other person, we shared our thoughts in small groups. We then took our break for lunch.

When we returned to the seminar that afternoon, we were asked to review in our minds what we despised about the other person. The leader then suggested that it was very likely that the reason for our hostile feelings was that the very characteristics which we despised in the other person were actually reflections of our own shadow side. It was suggested that the reason we react to this kind of person is that we have never become honest with God about our own shadow side. Each of us are weak and flawed in certain aspects of our character. None of us are perfect as Jesus was perfect. The more honest we become about our shadow side, the more it sets us free to quit reacting to those who have these same characteristics.

I have heard such things before. I know that this is generally true. I was not overly shocked at the reminder that I have a shadow side in my life which must be intentionally faced. However, I was not ready for what the seminar leader did next. We were each given a large sheet of paper. On one side of the sheet we were told to write the characteristics for which we feel genuine and legitimate pride. Most of the pastors wrote such words as *caring, trustworthy, patient,* and *nurturing*. Then, we were told to write all those characteristics we had identified in the person we despised. Lists included such words as *arrogant, moody, careless,* and *judgmental*. After taking time to write out both lists, we were then given masking tape and asked to wear the positive sides of ourselves for the others in the seminar to see. We spent several minutes wandering around the room reading each other's signs and affirming each other's strengths. Then came the hard part. We were next told to wear the list which identified our shadow side. With some genuine embarrassment we wandered around the room and read each other's statements of what we dislike in our lives and what we try to hide from ourselves and others.

Actually it was not so bad to do this activity in a group of clergy who do not know each other and will likely never see each other again. I was thinking, however, what would happen if I led such an exercise in our own congregation. Some of us have a great deal of difficulty being honest about our positive points and offering our gifts as a blessing to others. Others of us have more trouble facing our shadow sides. If you had to write two lists, what would each list include? This is what I think would happen if we wore such signs identifying both our strengths and our shadow sides. I think our closest friends already know. I suspect our closest friends and family already know even those shadow aspects of our character which we think we have carefully hidden. I suspect the only ones we are fooling are ourselves. God already knows us as we really are. Our family and closest friends already know some of our worst shadow aspects. Isn't it time we came clean and admitted the truth to ourselves? The spiritual discipline of confession often means we are finally confessing the truth to ourselves.

Several years ago I read an interesting article in *Psychology Today*. While I did not save it and do not remember the author or date, I do recall the basic content of the article. The writer was describing what had happened to Vietnam veterans who had returned to the United States and had become deeply depressed. The article mentioned that we lost more Vietnam veterans after the end of the war than in the actual battles. Many Vietnam veterans returned home with feelings of unresolved guilt. While many of these veterans sought counseling, few felt any relief as a result of the counseling. The drug overdoses and suicides continued at a shocking rate over the next years. Why were the counselors unable to help these Vietnam veterans?

The author identified the early style of counseling used with returning Vietnam War veterans. When the young man would admit that he had killed innocent women and children in the midst of the uncertainties of the Vietnam situation, the counselors would often respond that this was understandable and justifiable. After all, this was war and innocent people are bound to be injured. When the veterans described recurring nightmares, the counselors tried to explain that such occurrences were entirely acceptable since there were no good choices and that all that was left was the lesser of wrongs. Still the suicides, overdoses and violent eruptions continued.

The article then concluded that the counseling approach had not helped these Vietnam veterans because it failed to assist the young men in facing up to their own shadow sides. The article suggested that we might have done better with these returning vets if we had helped them admit their legitimate guilt and come to deeper levels of honesty with their failings. The author concluded that confession of evil and acceptance of forgiveness bring health while continuing to justify one's wrong actions fails to bring any sense of resolution.

I think Dr. Scott Peck has delved more deeply into the importance of confession than any other author I have read. In his book *People of the Lie*, Dr. Peck defines evil people as those who are unable to admit their sins. He says that feeling genuinely guilty over actual wrongs is a blessing since it keeps us from becoming truly evil people. Only those who fail to admit their shadow sides are in danger of true evil. Dr. Peck writes about evil people in this way, "...the central defect of the evil is not the sin but the refusal to acknowledge it."[1] A few paragraphs later Dr. Peck comments that people who are "blessed by guilt," are the ones who manage to turn away from evil.

Are we people who are "blessed by guilt?" The spiritual discipline of confession helps us avoid becoming evil people. Evil happens when we lie to ourselves and to God. The spiritual discipline of confession is about our being brutally honest. I suspect the reason we avoid such deep levels of honesty is that we think we are alone in our struggles with certain sins. We worry that if others knew what we have thought and done, they would be horrified at us. It is my experience in counseling parishioners that there are no new sins under the sun. Regardless of our character flaws or whatever our secret sins may be, others in this congregation have struggled with the same things.

I have lost count of how many church members have confessed to me their failings to remain faithful to their marriage vows. I do not recall how many women in our church have struggled with guilt over abortions of the past. We have among us people who have served time in prison, people who have born children out of wedlock, people who have cheated their companies, people who have been dishonest in their financial dealings; the list goes on and on. Yet we sit in our pews each Sunday and do not realize that in this fine-looking, relatively affluent congregation are seriously wounded people. One of the first things I tell someone, when they finally come to my study and want to make a confession to God, is that they are not alone.

One of the best things about the spiritual discipline of confession is that it helps break our isolation. When we think we were all alone with our guilt, we discover that others not only have shared these same struggles but also have discovered healing through honesty.

Walter Wangerin, a Lutheran author, recalls the time his unconfessed sin had left him with disastrous feelings of isolation. Walter Wangerin's father was the president of a Lutheran college in Canada. Every summer when he was a young boy, Walter and other faculty children used to play soccer games in a grassy field on the college campus. While the summer grassy field was ideal for playing in stocking feet, every so often the game would be halted for a boy to pitch a stone, which had risen to the surface during the winter. Walter's favorite technique was to throw the stone at one of the huge lights overlooking the field used for hockey in the winter. Walter knew he would never hit a light with his poor aim, but it made a fun sport anyway.

One day as Walter aimed a stone at a lightbulb, his father's angry voice rang out nearby, "Wally! What are you doing?" "Nothing," yelled back Walter. "*Wally!*" exclaimed his father. No matter how he tried to convince his father that he could never actually hit a lightbulb with his poor aim, his father forbade him to throw stones at the expensive lights. Near the end of the summer Walter pitched a stone at a lightbulb, perhaps one of the last stones to be thrown from the field that August, and hit his target. The lightbulb burst, and the glass tinkled to the ground. Walter turned on his brother and friends and made them promise never to tell.

Thus began Walter's feelings of isolation because of unconfessed sin. His father, not knowing the misdeed, continued to greet his son in a normal, cheerful voice. He continued to call his son by a favorite nickname Ah-vee. Walter no longer felt like he deserved to be loved by his father. His heart ached every time his father called him the name since he no longer felt worthy of being called Ah-vee.

The isolation happening between Walter and his father was also between Walter and his brother. In a rage at his brother for laughing at him, Walter recalls punching his own brother hard enough to actually hurt him. This was something he had never done before. Then, he writes what he realized about himself: "I saw the great hurt I'd given him, and the great evil that I had become, and I hated myself."

Walter Wangerin describes himself as "...caught between loneliness and corporal punishment." He was hesitant to admit the truth to his father, yet he realized what his refusal to be honest was doing to him. Thus, he made the decision to go tell his father what he had done. Walter walked down the long hall to his father's office. He stood before the huge, oak door and fearfully knocked. "Come in," his father said as he remained seated behind the desk and then queried, "Well?" Hesitantly, Walter began to make his confession. "You know those six-thousand-watt lightbulbs at the rink?" "Yes," replied his father. "Well, I broke one," confessed Walter. He hesitated and then finally included in his admission that the lightbulb had been broken by his throwing a stone.

Walter Wangerin's father rose from behind the desk and slowly came toward him. Walter stiffened in preparation for the deserved spanking. It would feel better to get it over with after having worried about his father's anger for so long. Walter had convinced himself that he would not cry when spanked. However, he was not ready for what happened next. Walter's father knelt down and took him in his arms and hugged him. As Walter collapsed into tears, he recalls his father whispering softly, "Ah-vee, Ah-vee."[2]

God's response to us in the discipline of confession is as surprising as Walter Wangerin's experience with his father. We expect God's legitimate anger. We fear God will turn away from us in horror at our sins. Actually the opposite is what happens. God wraps us in loving arms and whispers to us that we are understood, valued, loved, and forgiven.

A little Filipino girl said that Jesus appeared to her and talked with her. When her fellow villagers became convinced that her experiences were authentic, the bishop in Manila was told about her. The bishop became somewhat concerned and assigned a monsignor to investigate the situation.

The girl was brought to the bishop's palace for a series of diagnostic interviews. Finally, after several conversations the monsignor was still uncertain as to whether or not her experiences were genuine. So he came up with a test. The monsignor said to the girl, "The next time you talk to Jesus, I want you to ask him what I confessed at my last confession. Would you do that?" The girl agreed and went back to her village. The next week she returned to speak with the monsignor. He asked whether she had talked with Jesus and asked the question. She responded that she had. "Well?" asked the monsignor, "When you asked Jesus what I confessed to at my last confession, what did Jesus say?" The little girl answered, "Jesus said, 'I've forgotten.'"[3]

Of course, this was the right answer. The wonderful thing about the spiritual discipline of confession is that our confession is made to our forgetful Lord. God wraps loving arms around us, and the very next day God does not even remember what it was that we confessed. We are free to move on with our lives. It is no wonder that this spiritual discipline is so central to our continued healing as we become the people who live our lives by the motto: What would Jesus do?

---

[1]M. Scott Peck, M.D., *People of the Lie: the Hope for Healing Human Evil* (New York: Simon and Schuster, Inc., 1983) 69.

[2]Walter Wangerin, Jr., *The Manger Is Empty* (San Fransisco: Harper and Row, 1989) 164-171.

[3]M. Scott Peck, M.D., *Further Along the Road Less Traveled* (New York: Simon and Schuster, 1993) 158-159.

The Discipline of Faith

Now faith is the assurance of things hoped for, the conviction of things not seen.

Hebrews 11:1

Now when Jesus returned, the crowd welcomed him, for they were all waiting for him. And there came a man named Jairus, who was a ruler of the synagogue; and falling at Jesus' feet he besought him to come to his house, for he had an only daughter, about twelve years of age, and she was dying.

As he went, the people pressed round him. And a woman who had had a flow of blood for twelve years and could not be healed by any one came up behind him, and touched the fringe of his garment; and immediately her flow of blood ceased. And Jesus said, "Who was it that touched me?" When all denied it, Peter said, "Master the multitudes surround you and press upon you!" But Jesus said, "Some one touched me; for I perceive that power has gone forth from me." And when the woman saw that she was not hidden, she came trembling, and falling down before him declared in the presence of all the people why she had touched him, and how she had been immediately healed. And he said to her, "Daughter, your faith has made you well; go in peace."

While he was still speaking, a man from the ruler's house came and said, "Your daughter is dead; do not trouble the Teacher anymore." But Jesus on hearing this answered him, "Do not fear; only believe, and she shall be well." And when he came to the house, he permitted no one to enter with him, except Peter and John and

*James, and the father and mother of the child. And all were weeping
and bewailing her; but he said, "Do not weep; for she is not dead
but sleeping." And they laughed at him, knowing that she was
dead. But taking her by the hand he called, saying, "Child, arise."
And her spirit returned, and she got up at once; and he directed
that something should be given her to eat. And her parents were
amazed; but he charged them to tell no one what had happened.*

Luke 8:40-56

These last few weeks some people have commented to me
that they could see some of these same spiritual disciplines
overlapping the Twelve Step recovery programs such as Alcoholics
Anonymous. Indeed, many of these same spiritual disciplines are
intentionally part of the Twelve Step recovery programs. In fact,
the spiritual discipline of faith is central to the Twelve Steps.

To be honest, I seriously considered simply returning to the
series of sermons I preached a few years ago on the Twelve Steps
and using updated examples to merely preach those sermons again.
However, I decided instead to focus on the spiritual disciplines of
Jesus' life since there are several spiritual disciplines which are not
included in the Twelve Step programs. For instance, the Twelve
Steps do not include the spiritual disciplines of Bible study or
submission. While the Twelve Steps can be very effective in
helping people recover from addictive behavior, they are not
intended specifically to help people become more like Jesus. Since
our goal in this series of messages is to discover what Jesus would
do in our situations, it seemed appropriate to focus on the
disciplines which Jesus demonstrated.

Let us begin our considerations by defining the spiritual
discipline of faith. The writer of Hebrews said, "Faith is being sure
of what we hope for and certain of what we do not see" (Hebrews
11:1). Perhaps one of the most common misunderstandings about
Christianity is the idea that faith is difficult. Many people seem to
think that they do not have enough faith to follow Jesus Christ. I
would suggest that we already have plenty of faith. Jesus said if we
have as much faith as a tiny mustard seed, it is enough to do what

God wants us to do (Luke 17:6). Mustard seeds are so minute that hundreds of them can fit on the tip of a finger. If anything, our problem is that faith comes too easily. So why do we call faith a spiritual discipline? What needs to be disciplined about faith?

A man met with his psychiatrist for his first appointment. When the psychiatrist asked why he needed help, the man proceeded to explain that his wife and friends felt he needed counseling. The man explained, "I know that I am dead and you know that I am dead, but my wife and friends insist that I am not dead." The psychiatrist listened for an hour as the man explained that he was dead. At the end of their time the doctor made an appointment to meet again with him in two weeks. Then the psychiatrist gave the man an assignment before their next meeting. The psychiatrist told the man to recite a simple statement to himself at least ten times a day. The statement was the following: Dead people do not bleed.

Two weeks later the man returned for his second appointment. The psychiatrist asked if he had been reciting the assigned statement. Yes, at least ten times a day the man had repeated to himself that dead people do not bleed. Then the psychiatrist took the man's hand and with a needle pricked the man's finger. The doctor squeezed out a drop of blood and waited as the man took in this information about himself. After a moment's pause the man excitedly declared, "Hey, look doc, dead people *do* bleed!"

Faith is a strange thing. If we are not careful to practice faith as a spiritual discipline, we can find ourselves believing almost anything. The problem of faith is not quantity; we already have enough faith: The concern is quality. We need to be disciplined about what we trust and how we use our faith.

Jesus knew that people's faith could heal them. He also knew that a room filled with faith could bring the dead back. Jesus understood that faith is so powerful that it needs to be disciplined.

Scientists have appreciated the fact for years that faith is amazingly powerful. In the 1600's Robert Boyle became an outstanding natural scientist and a leader in the field of chemistry. He went into the field of chemistry because of a boyhood experience. While away at school, Robert became so ill that the school doctor was called. The doctor prescribed medication. When the pharmacist delivered the medication to the family where young Robert was living, a servant girl prepared the potion and gave it to Robert. The result was disastrous. There was a mix-up and the wrong medication had been delivered to the wrong address. Young Robert Boyle almost died. The physician spent an entire day sitting at the boy's bedside, nursing him back to health.

Some months later when Robert became sick a second time, the same servant girl sniffed the medication which had been delivered and decided to throw it away. Instead of the medicine she poured some prune juice into a cup and served it to the boy. Robert Boyle screwed up his face and fought the gag reflex as he swallowed the drink. "That stuff tastes awful!", he shrieked. However, by that evening he was feeling significantly better. He told the servant girl that whatever the medicine was, it had worked very well. She admitted that it was nothing more than plain prune juice. "Prune juice!", Robert wondered aloud. "Then, why did it taste so bad?" He concluded that he had expected a bad medicinal taste, so he had tricked his own taste buds. Then, he began considering whether the reason he felt so much better might not be the same reason. He expected to get better and indeed was healed because of his faith more than by an actual medication. Robert Boyle had discovered the power of faith. The placebo of prune juice was as effective as an actual medicine because he believed in it.[1]

A placebo is something used in place of actual medicine. A placebo is used when the doctor feels that the patient needs mental healing and faith more than actual chemical treatment of the ailment. In the 1600's there was little awareness of the power of faith to effect healing through placebos. Since then, we have documented the power of faith through placebos to bring healing.

Norman Cousins in his book *The Anatomy of an Illness* devotes an entire chapter to placebos. Cousins recognizes the fact that placebos can assist a person toward a healing experience by drawing on the power of faith. He cites a number of studies. For instance, the late Henry K. Beecher, a noted Harvard anesthesiologist, performed fifteen different studies of placebos with more than 1,000 patients. Dr. Beecher concluded that 35% of patients experienced satisfactory relief when given a placebo.

One specific study involved the treatment of postoperative wound pain. Drs. Beecher and Lasagna alternated morphine with a placebo treatment. After a dose of morphine the recovering patients would be given a placebo treatment, then morphine, then the placebo. The placebo was 77% as effective as the morphine.

Another study of placebos was done by medical officials in the National Institute of Geriatrics in Romania. Scientists were studying a new drug intended to activate the endocrine system in order to enhance health and extend life. In order to accurately test the new drug, they designed a double-blind test. One hundred and fifty people were divided into three groups of fifty. The first group was given no medication. The second group was given a placebo. The third group was given the new test drug. Year by year they continued the study. The results, years later, were that the first group showed the same death rate as fellow villagers. The second group, which received placebos, showed a marked lengthening of life, an improvement of health, and a measurably lower death rate than fellow villagers. The third group, on the new experimental drug, did even better than the placebo group.

The scientific evidence is clear about one thing: Placebos really work! They work because of the power of faith. Norman Cousins concludes his chapter on placebos by describing his meeting with Dr. Albert Schweitzer in Africa. As the two men were walking through the Schweitzer hospital in Lambarene, Cousins commented on the break-through of modern medicine so that the people no longer needed to rely on witch doctors. Dr. Schweitzer responded by inviting Norman Cousins to come to a ceremony where a witch doctor was at work.

The two men watched as the patients came to the witch doctor. With some of the patients the witch doctor performed a chant and ritual. With others he brewed an herbal tea mixture for them to take at home. For some the witch doctor whispered into their ears and pointed over to Dr. Schweitzer, encouraging them to go to the hospital for surgery. On the way back to the hospital, Dr. Schweitzer explained that his practice and the witch doctor's complimented each other. Frequently patients were referred back and forth between the two. Dr. Schweitzer explained that the success rate of the witch doctor was about the same as his own success rate with patients.

Witch doctors understand the psychology of illness and health. Many people have genuine physical problems which are a result of emotional problems. For these situations the witch doctor is as effective in healing as the medical physician. Dr. Schweitzer explained to Norman Cousins, "The witch doctor succeeds for the same reason all the rest of us succeed. Each patient carries his own doctor inside him." Thus, Norman Cousins concludes the chapter, "The placebo is the doctor who resides within."[2]

I was a young Christian when I first experienced this power of faith. In my junior year of college I blew out my right knee in a gymnastic accident. I ruined all the cartilage and tore the cruciate ligaments. I went straight from the gymnasium to the doctor's office where the physician was able to twist my knee in such a way that my lower leg stood out to the side as I lay flat on the examining table. Within a couple of hours I was in surgery.

I recall the next few days in the hospital. The doctor would check on me and say that all was going well. The nurses were caring, and my family was supportive during my recovery. I assumed all was well and that I was holding up as expected. Then, I think it was near the end of the second day, one of the nurses made an off-hand remark that changed my expectations. She commented on my amazing ability to manage pain, stating that this was normally a painful recovery but that I had never even asked for a pain pill or shot in the first two days. What the nurse did not know was that no one had told me that I was supposed to be in pain. I did not know that I could request pain medication. As soon as I learned of this expectation, I was writhing in pain within a half hour. I felt silly calling for the nurse and asking for pain medication when I had felt no pain up to that point.

The fact that I walk without a limp is largely due to the power of faith. After my cast was removed, I began intensive therapy to get my atrophied leg back into shape. Over the next six months one of my college friends, a fellow gymnast, constantly harped at me about my continuing limp. He insisted that I force myself to walk without a limp. Six months after the surgery I was not only walking without a limp but also able to compete again as a gymnast. What I did not know until later was that the surgeon had confided to my parents that the injury would end my career as a gymnast and that I would most likely have a limp the rest of my life. Fortunately neither the doctor nor my parents told me so that my faith could cure beyond what medical science might have expected.

Faith is amazing; faith is powerful. Jesus knew that a woman was healed simply by faith without his needing to help her faith at all. In fact, when Jesus stopped the entire crowd to instruct the woman that her faith had healed her, he very likely was helping her avoid an error in her understanding of what had just happened. Can you imagine what she might have told others if Jesus had not instructed her about faith? She might have gone home and told her family and friends that she had touched Jesus' cloak to become well. People might have thought there was some special power in the cloth and even begun to worship the fabric rather than realizing the power of faith.

When Jesus entered the home where a girl had recently died, he insisted that only those with faith remain in his presence as he called the girl back to life. The rest of the crowd was dismissed since their skepticism and lack of faith could endanger Jesus' healing power. Jesus taught the disciples that faith of an individual can be magnified when it is in the presence of the faith of others. On the other hand, when some in the group believed she was dead, and others believe she is sleeping and can be raised, the conflict can nullify the positive faith of even Jesus himself.

This brings us to the most important reason that faith must be treated as a spiritual discipline. Faith can build or it can destroy. It can heal or it can hurt. Faith alone is neither good nor bad. What makes faith good depends on that in which we put our faith. When we treat faith as a spiritual discipline, we are reminded that faith must be coordinated with the other spiritual disciplines in order to help us become more like Jesus.

Let us remember that the spiritual disciplines are intended to work together. One spiritual discipline needs the others in order to keep us balanced as we seek to walk in the footsteps of Jesus Christ. If we practice the spiritual discipline of submission without the accompanying discipline of service, we can end up with a manipulative cult leader such as Jim Jones, pulling followers out of the world. Thus, this spiritual discipline becomes a twisted, unhealthy version of what it was meant to be. We can even end up with cult followers blindly obeying whatever the leader says, even drinking poison.

The spiritual discipline of faith must be combined with the spiritual discipline of study in order for both to be beneficial. Through the discipline of study we become aware of God's truth. Through the discipline of faith we learn to put God's truth into action in everyday life.

Dr. Francis Schaeffer, a missionary in Switzerland until his death a few years ago, had a wonderful illustration of the importance of combining the disciplines of faith and study. Arguing that Jesus never wanted people to practice gullible, blind faith, Dr. Schaeffer used to use this analogy from his time in the Swiss Alps.

Suppose a group of mountain climbers become caught in a thick, evening fog so that they are no longer able to proceed without serious danger of falling over a cliff. The guide explains how serious the situation is by letting them know that if they do not get off the shoulder of the mountain they will all freeze to death. However, with such heavy fog it is dangerous to proceed. Imagine that one of the climbers asks the guide, "If I climb out onto the ledge and then hang and drop, is it possible that there is a ledge a few feet down which might catch me and protect me through the night?" When the guide explains it is possible, though not particularly likely, then the person simply drops into the dense fog with the hope of hitting a possible ledge. While this could be called faith, it is clearly not the spiritual discipline of faith as Jesus practiced it.

Suppose, however, that a voice calls out through the fog. The voice tells the climbers that he is on a neighboring ridge, has seen their plight, and wants to help. He assures them that he knows the Alps well and is certain that there is a ledge beneath them, which they can find by inching out to the edge and hanging and dropping.

Is this enough information to justify obeying the voice? No. This is a little better, but it still lacks the study component expected of Christians.

Dr. Schaeffer would conclude his example by describing the need to ask some questions of the voice in the fog. For instance, one might ask his name. In different parts of the Alps there are certain distinctive family names which could be identified as people who know their way through the mountains. Only after asking the questions necessary to determine the validity of the other person's knowledge is one justified in then hanging from the ledge in the faith that the helpful ledge will save him.[3]

Yes, we need faith. However, we already have enough faith to become the people God wants us to be. What we need is not more faith; what we need is the spiritual discipline of faith. As we learn to practice the combinations of the spiritual disciplines which Jesus exemplified, we will learn to walk in his steps.

---

[1] John Hudson Tiner, *Robert Boyle, Trailblazer of Science* (Milford: Mott Media, 1989) 36-37.

[2] Norman Cousins, *Anatomy of an Illness as Perceived by the Patient* (New York: Bantam, 1979) 69.

[3] Francis A. Schaeffer, *He Is There and He Is Not Silent* (Wheaton: Tyndale House, 1985) 99-100.

The Discipline of Patience

Be patient, therefore, brethren, until the coming of the Lord. Behold, the farmer waits for the precious fruit of the earth, being patient over it until it receives the early and the late rain. You also be patient. Establish your hearts, for the coming of the Lord is at hand.

James 5:7-8

Now they had forgotten to bring bread; and they had only one loaf with them in the boat. And he cautioned them, saying, "Take heed, beware of the leaven of the Pharisees and the leaven of Herod." And they discussed it with one another, saying, "We have no bread." And being aware of it, Jesus said to them, "Why do you discuss the fact that you have no bread? Do you not yet perceive or understand? Are your hearts hardened? Having eyes do you not see, and having ears do you not hear? And do you not remember? When I broke the five loaves for the five thousand, how many baskets full of broken pieces did you take up?" They said to him, "Twelve." "And the seven for the four thousand, how many baskets full of broken pieces did you take up?" And they said to him, "Seven." And he said to them, "Do you not yet understand?"

Mark 8:14-21

Presbyterians do not talk about predestination much anymore. This week we received our first long-distance phone call from our second son, who is now attending Northern Arizona University in

Flagstaff. After the excitement of telling us how he had arranged his dorm room, and had been running into old friends around campus, he shifted the conversation to theology. "Dad, I met this Baptist girl who says that God predestines who will be saved and who will go to hell. She gave me some Bible verses to read, and I am trying to defend what Presbyterians believe about predestination. Can you help me?"

For the next twenty minutes we discussed various interpretations of the biblical passages regarding predestination. Justus found one thought in particular most helpful. I reminded him that the sentence in Romans 8:29 is frequently left unfinished and thus confused. I have heard this verse quoted as though there were a period after the word *predestined.* "For those whom God fore-knew, God also predestined." This is a misquote. We need to read the rest of the sentence. "For those whom God fore-knew, God also predestined to be conformed to the image of God's Son in order that Jesus might be the firstborn in a large family." Predestination teaches us what the goal of a Christian's life is to be. We are to become more and more like Jesus, our big brother. God's predestined goal for us is to become like Christ.

Becoming like Christ involves constant growth and change. The theological word for this ongoing process of change toward godliness is *sanctification.* I want us to think about sanctification today as we consider the ongoing process of change.

A prosperous executive decided to buy a small plane so that he could fly from city to city on his own schedule. He enjoyed flying so much that after a few years he decided to also purchase a pontoon plane to fly directly to his summer cabin on a lake.

On his first flight to the lake in his new plane he forgot and headed for the small, airport landing strip just as he had always done. Luckily his wife was with him. When the plane was just a few feet off the ground, she screamed, "Wait! Pull up! You can't land on the runway. This plane has pontoons instead of tires!"

At the last minute the man lifted the plane back up into the sky, circled over the lake, and came in for a safe landing on the water. As he shut the engine off, he turned to his wife and said, "I don't know what I was thinking. That is one of the stupidest things

I have ever done!" Then he opened the door and stepped out into the lake.

Change is never easy. Sanctification involves work. The spiritual disciplines are given by God to help us in this continuous process of becoming the people God wants us to be.

We saw last time that the spiritual disciplines need to be combined and balanced in order to keep us growing toward Christ's likeness. This is particularly true when it comes to the spiritual discipline of patience. All of the other disciplines are practically worthless if we are not willing to practice patience and persistence in order to let the change toward godliness happen over a period of time.

One of the first letdowns in my youthful Christianity was the realization that God does not always change us miraculously. When I became a Christian during my first year of college, I understood the promise of Scripture to say that I was a completely new person in Christ. I assumed that meant God would do all the changes for me and all that I had to do was sit back and watch God work in my life. While a few changes occurred miraculously, most of the changes in my life have involved effort and discipline on my part.

One of the miraculous changes that occurred when I became a Christian was a dramatic shift in my vocabulary on the gymnastics team. Before I knew Christ, I had quite a reputation for being foulmouthed. I did not use such words in the presence of women nor around my family, but I thought that cussing up a storm was part of the ambiance of athletics during team practices. Shortly after I received Jesus as my Lord and Savior, I realized that I no longer needed to use such words as the Spirit of God painlessly removed any desire to cuss. I honestly had not realized how bad my language had been until team-mates began asking me what happened to me that I had changed so dramatically. They noticed the change and commented to me that I was much more fun to be around at practices when I was not using such foul language.

I naively thought all of Christian life would be that easy. I expected to simply pray and ask God to forgive my past sins and release me from any future temptations, and sanctification would happen just as easily as the cussing had dropped away. I did not yet understand that sanctification takes work. Over the next twenty years of my life I would enter the process of sanctification by learning the discipline of patience.

The Bible is full of examples of God's people having to grow through patience. Abraham had to learn the spiritual discipline of patience. He was ninety years old and his wife was eighty when Sarah gave up hoping for the conception of a son. Thus, Abraham conceived a son through Sarah's servant woman Hagar. Still, God told Abraham that his wife Sarah would bear a son. Abraham was ninety-nine years old and his wife Sarah was nearly ninety when God repeated the promise which they had heard for years but had seen no evidence of the promise's fulfillment. No wonder they laughed at the idea of becoming parents at their age. Yet God would bring about a miraculous conception in their old age if they were willing to be patient (Genesis 17). How many of us would have waited on God's promise and believed that God could make us parents in our nineties?

Joseph sat in jail in Egypt. His brothers had sold him into slavery and then his owner's wife made a false accusation which sent him to prison. Joseph did not know it yet, but God was teaching him the spiritual discipline of patience. While Joseph sat in prison, God was arranging the affairs of Egypt so that in future years Joseph would be in the right place at the right time to save his family's lives. He did not know it in prison, but someday he would rule as Pharaoh's assistant. In the meantime Joseph practiced the daily disciplines of prayer and meditation. He studied dreams and learned the Egyptian culture. When the time was right, God would redeem all Joseph's suffering into something good. But first, he had to wait in prison and learn the spiritual discipline of patience (Genesis 40).

Someday Moses would lead the Israelites out of slavery. However, the Pharaoh's heart was still hardened against God. Escape from Egypt would not happen quickly or easily. First, there would be the convincing of his fellow Israelites that he was indeed called to lead them. Next, there would be ten plagues of judgment against Egypt before the Pharaoh would release the Israelite slaves.

The bondage in Egypt would get worse before it got it better. God was teaching Moses and Israel the spiritual discipline of patience through this process (Exodus 4-12).

Elijah announced that there would be a drought as God's judgment against Israel's unfaithfulness. Then he departed as instructed by God's Spirit. He lived for several months in a wilderness place eating food brought by ravens and drinking from a nearby stream. Then something happened. The stream dried up due to the lack of rain. Even Elijah himself was suffering along with the rest of God's people. He ventured into a nearby town and asked a widow for a handout. She explained that she was nearly out of food due to the drought. She was just getting ready to prepare the last meal for herself and her son before they starved to death. Elijah prayed, and the food lasted over the next days and months until the famine and drought were ended. Elijah and the widow learned patience (I Kings 17).

The Apostle Paul experienced a dramatic conversion while he was on the road to Damascus. Soon after becoming a Christian, Paul began to preach to his fellow Jews in Damascus. His early sermons brought little more than anger and an assassination attempt on his life. Thus, he disappeared into the Arabian desert for a few years. We do not know what happened to Paul during his lost desert years. It is likely that he was learning the spiritual disciplines which he would need to become the apostle to the Roman Empire. One thing is sure: He must have learned the spiritual discipline of patience as he spent those years away from the public eye (Galatians 1:17-18).

Show me any great person of God, and I will show you someone who has had to learn the spiritual discipline of patience. Sanctification takes time and does not happen easily. Becoming God's person is a long, arduous process. Why doesn't God simply solve our problems overnight? While there are probably many reasons God chooses to work in this way, I suspect one reason is that our lessons during the process of sanctification can become an example to others.

My sister-in-law Virginia has spent years teaching in federal and state prison systems. Her focus has been on teaching prisoners how to earn a G.E.D. (The General Equivalency Diploma is granted to those who have dropped out of high school and then completed required course work in order to be considered graduated from high school.) Virginia takes the students from very basic levels of reading, science, and math to the necessary requirements for high school competency. I understand that she is very good at what she does and particularly good at teaching basic math skills toward the G.E.D.

The reason I find this interesting is that my sister-in-law is miserable at math. For example, we were once playing a game of Yahtzee together as a family. Virginia rolled the five dice, and they came up with four five's and a three. She decided to use the four five's for her score on that play. I watched and listened as she added her total. She counted by five's, "Five, ten, fifteen." Then she paused and leaned down close to the fourth five and continued counting the little dots, "Sixteen, seventeen, eighteen, nineteen, twenty." This is poor math! Most third graders can recite the multiplication table for five's.

Virginia laughs when we recall her struggles with the dice while playing Yahtzee. She comments, "That is why I am such a good math teacher for the G.E.D. My math is so bad that I have to take the examples slowly and systematically." The poorest student can follow her explanations because she also has problems with math.

Along with this first reason for God's teaching us the spiritual discipline of patience, a second comes to mind. Could it be that having to learn our lessons slowly helps us to appreciate our neighbor's struggles to walk with Christ? When we have learned through patience, we become less judgmental in our attitudes.

I generally do not have much trouble with my weight. Many of my friends tease me about eating such hearty meals while still not seeming to put on any weight. Perhaps it is my metabolism. To be honest, I used to have difficulty understanding and appreciating the struggles of those who struggle with their weight. That is until a few summers ago. Our family went on an extended two-week vacation to Idaho. The combination of sitting in the van most of the day and eating snacks most of the time left me by the end of the trip astonished to discover that I was twenty pounds heavier than I had ever been.

My first reaction was to simply try and take off the extra pounds as quickly as they had gone on. I figured I could simply ride the exercise bike a few extra miles and cut back on the calories for a week or two and everything would be back to normal. The first week I lost five pounds. However, I quickly gained four of them back. I then lost seven pounds, gaining five back. For the first time the weight did not simply melt off as it had in the past. As my frustration increased, my wife gave me some wise advice when she said, "Bruce, crash diets do not work because they do not solve the problem. You are going to have to change some of the lifestyle habits of your past. You cannot continue to eat ice cream at 10:00 at night and expect the weight to stay off like it did when you were a gymnast." In fact, she maintains, and I suspect she is right, that I simply had not weighed myself for several months prior to the vacation, so the weight had crept up without my noticing and was not a sudden increase over just a two-week period.

I still have a much easier time with my weight than most people. However, I am learning in my middle-age years that I must be more careful than I have in the past. The answer is not a crash diet; it is daily discipline. The answer for most of our problems is not some quick, easy solution.

We often do not respect the power of the little daily things to make a difference. We are enamored of the huge, dramatic events of life which seem so life-changing. Actually most of our lives are changed in minute ways through a disciplined series of small, seemingly insignificant steps.

Victor Hugo, in his famous novel *The Hunchback of Notre-Dame* has a classic discussion contrasting the huge dramatic things with the small. A priest is reflecting on the traditional way the church taught faith through architecture and art. Huge cathedrals with biblical scenes in stained-glass windows and their facades with gargoyles and saints had helped the illiterate masses to understand God's call. However, with the advent of the printing press some major changes took place. Something as small as a tract or book, printed in such small letters, had the capacity to destroy people's former faith. The archdeacon in the story says, "Alas! the small things shall bring down the great things; a tooth triumphs over a whole carcass; the rat of the Nile destroys the crocodile; the swordfish kills the whale; the book will kill the edifice."[1]

> Humpty Dumpty sat on a wall.
> Humpty Dumpty had a great fall.
> All the king's horses and all the king's men
> Couldn't put Humpty back together again.

What ever happened to Humpty Dumpty? Years ago a Presbyterian turned this nursery rhyme into a marvelous parable of sanctification. Let me paraphrase his story.

The King decided to take matters into his own hand. He took off his robe, replaced his royal garments with common peasant's clothing, and slipped through the palace gates to go search for Humpty. After several days and nights the persistent king found Humpty's shattered body in a back alley. The king ran to Humpty and cried, "Humpty! It is I, your King! I am here to help!"

Humpty turned away. "Leave me alone! I have gotten used to living here. I don't mind it so much anymore. In fact, I kind of like this new way of life. I can eat the scraps that others toss. The garbage can sparkles at certain times in the morning when the sun hits it just right and is actually quite beautiful. I don't need your help."

The King assured Humpty that there were many beautiful places in the kingdom which he could never know if he remained satisfied in his broken condition. Humpty grumbled that he had no need for the King.

Some days later Humpty opened his bleary eyes and saw the face of the king bowing over him. "I have come to help," the King said.

"Leave me alone," said Humpty. "My psychiatrist says that I am doing fine. I have adjusted to my environment. You are living in a dreamworld. I live in reality right here in the alley."

"Wouldn't you rather walk?" the King asked.

"If I get up and start walking, I will have to change everything else. I am simply not ready to make the kind of commitment it takes to be a walker. I have learned to accept my broken condition; why can't you?"

For more than a year Humpty remained in his broken condition, refusing to let the king do anything. Then one day Humpty opened his eyes to see the king coming toward him yet again. Somehow this time it seemed different. Humpty greeted the king in a positive, hopeful way. When the king made his offer, Humpty decided to give it a try. He let the king pick up the broken pieces of his life and begin piecing together the fragments. After a great deal of work the king lifted Humpty to a standing position. Wobbly at first, Humpty took his first steps since the accident.

The king then began a slow but regular regimen of walking with Humpty. Each day the two would walk a little further together. Pretty soon they were taking walks along beautiful beaches and enjoying green mountain pastures. They would laugh and converse as they walked together. They became best friends.

Then one day it happened. What the king had hoped for and believed could happen had in fact occurred. As the two were walking through a city in the kingdom, they overheard someone ask the question, "Who are those two men?"

The following answer was given, "I don't know the one on the right. But the one on the left is Humpty Dumpty. As much as they look and walk alike, I bet the other is old Humpty's brother!"[2]

We are predestined to walk with Jesus and talk with Jesus until people see the likeness. It takes patience, but the goal is to become sisters and brothers of Jesus Christ.

[1] Victor Hugo, *The Hunchback of Notre-Dame: A New Translation* by Walter J. Cobb (New York: Penguin Books/Signet Classic, 1965) 173.

[2] Vic Pentz, "Humpty Dumpty Revisited," *The Wittenburg Door* June 1972.

The Discipline of Reconciliation

Therefore, if any one is in Christ, he is a new creation; the old has passed away, behold, the new has come. All this is from God, who through Christ reconciled us to himself and gave us the ministry of reconciliation; that is, God was in Christ reconciling the world to himself, not counting their trespasses against them, and entrusting to us the message of reconciliation. So we are ambassadors for Christ, God making his appeal through us. We beseech you on behalf of Christ, be reconciled to God. For our sake he made him to be sin who knew no sin, so that in him we might become the righteousness of God.

2 Corinthians 5:17-21

So the soldiers did this. But standing by the cross of Jesus were his mother, and his mother's sister, Mary the wife of Clopas, and Mary Magdalene. When Jesus saw his mother, and the disciple whom he loved standing near, he said to his mother, "Woman, behold, your son!" Then he said to the disciple, "Behold, your mother!" And from that hour the disciple took her to his own home.

John 19:25-27

"Ours is an undisciplined age. The old disciplines are breaking down, and the foundations of society appear to be crumbling. The discipline of the home seems to be vanishing in the new psychology.... The old academic "disciplines": mathematics, ancient language, grammar, are being ignored as obsolete and unimportant. Above all, the disciplines of divine grace is derided as legalism or is entirely unknown to a generation that is largely illiterate in the Scriptures. We need the rugged strength of Christian character that can come only from discipline...."[1]

This quote sounds so contemporary that it comes almost as a shock to discover that it was written fifty years ago by a Christian of a previous generation. His concerns for our society were prophetic in their awareness of the direction of our nation. Even when the book *In His Steps* by Charles Sheldon was still the best-selling novel in America, the signs of a spiritually undisciplined Christianity were already clear. The decadence of our society has neither appeared overnight, nor will it be healed overnight.

It has been the contention of this summer's sermons on disciplines that if we asked ourselves, "What would Jesus do?" and tried to follow in his steps, not only would it turn our own lives around, it might even bring renewal to our nation. "What would Jesus do?" Among other things he would surely work for the reconciliation of broken relationships. He would forgive and help people be reconciled not only with God but also with each other. Let us consider the discipline of reconciliation.

A minister attended the wedding reception of a couple he had just married. The groom toasted the bride with the following words, "I want to start my marriage by being absolutely truthful with my bride. I need to admit to my bride and to everyone else here that I have spent many wonderful hours in the arms of another woman." Then after a brief pause for effect, the groom said, "She was my mother!"

The minister thought that he could use the same line to grab his congregation's attention for the next sermon. Thus, the minister stood before his congregation and began his sermon with these words, "I have a confession to make to my congregation and my wife. I need to admit that I have spent many wonderful hours in the arms of another woman." He paused for effect and then said, "But I can't for the life of me remember who she was!"

Misunderstandings can be humorous. They can also be hurtful. What if his confession had been real rather than a case of forgetfulness. Surely unfaithfulness and divorce are hurtful. A child's growing up in a broken home is not a laughing matter. It is sad that we live in a world of broken relationships. The sad truth is that we too often hurt the ones we love.

Most of us can relate to the moving scene in *Peter Pan* when jealous Tinker Bell tells the boys on the Island of the Lost Boys that Wendy is a dangerous bird who must be shot. As Wendy flies toward the Island of the Lost Boys, the boys begin to shoot arrows at her. The arrow of Tootles hits Wendy and knocks her out of the air. As the boys gather around the wounded Wendy Bird, they realize that this is the woman that Peter Pan has brought to be their mother. Tootles is most saddened by the realization of what he has done.

Tootles says, "I've always wanted a mother. I used to dream about a mother. In my dreams I would say, 'Oh my mother, oh my mother.' And then when she really came, I shot her."

Many of us have hurt someone we love. We wound each other through harsh words and hurtful acts. We take each other for granted or fail to meet each other's expectations. The result is the feeling of brokenness expressed by Tootles. What do we do about our broken relationships?

It is wonderful to be reminded that our sins are forgiven. As the Apostle Paul reminded the early Christians, "Be reconciled to God" (2 Corinthians 5:20). Jesus came to reconcile us to God by taking our sins on himself when he died on the cross. Jesus took our sin upon himself so that we might become new creations: we are cleansed and made new. This condition is the important starting place for the spiritual discipline of reconciliation. We cannot fully reconcile broken human relationships until we experience the personal reconciliation that Jesus offers.

Reconciliation with God, however, is just the start. As we learn to follow Jesus, we discover that Jesus wants us to pursue reconciliation with those we have hurt. Jesus, in the midst of the reconciling sacrifice on the cross, took some of the time on the cross to reconcile his disciples with his mother.

We sometimes forget that there had been some alienation and hurt feelings between Mary and the disciples. It hurt her feelings when she came to talk to Jesus and he refused to see her. When Jesus told the crowd that his disciples had taken the place of his mother and family, it must have deeply hurt her feelings. So when Jesus saw Mary and one of the disciples standing close to each other near the cross, he used the opportunity to bring healing and reconciliation. Jesus said to Mary, "Mother, behold your son!" And then he told the disciple, "Here is your mother." In other words, Jesus showed by his example that God cares about healing our broken relationships on earth as much as preparing us for heaven.

Let me suggest that the spiritual discipline of reconciliation involves three steps toward healing. First, we must stop the offending behavior. Second, we must offer a genuine apology. Third, we must forgive.

Most of us know the name of Will Rogers. A generation ago he reached a peak of popularity so that he was the highest paid entertainer in our country. In fact, a Broadway play was rewritten to include some lines by Will Rogers. The producers knew that the play would be an automatic success if Will Rogers' name were on the billboard. Their prediction was right. The play was a huge success. Then, during the fifth week the play suddenly was closed. Will Rogers was too busy with other commitments. This was the official reason given for closing the play. Years later, however, close friends of Will Rogers began to tell the rest of the story.

In the midst of the success of the play Will Rogers received a letter from a fan which made him stop and think about his participation in the play. The letter from a minister described his attendance at the theater with his fourteen-year-old daughter. Let me paraphrase the letter:

> Relying on you to give the public nothing that could bring the blush of shame to the cheeks of a Christian, I attended your performance with my fourteen-year-old daughter. However, I was deeply embarrassed when you did the scene in which the father lectures the son on the subject of his relations with an immoral woman. I took my

daughter by the hand, and we walked out. I haven't been able to look her in the eye since.[2]

Will Rogers was so upset by his actions having caused such an offense that he resigned from the play. While he personally saw nothing wrong with his part in the play, he took seriously his responsibility not to cause serious moral offense to others. Taking responsibility is the first step in the spiritual discipline of reconciliation. We will fail in our attempts at reconciliation if we refuse to recognize that our actions have indeed hurt others.

The second step in this spiritual discipline is the asking of forgiveness. When we own up to our fault and confess it to those we have hurt, it helps begin the healing process in their lives.

A few years after I left mission work among the Tlinget people of Alaska, I was impressed to hear that the Presbyterians had helped sponsor a service of reconciliation toward the native people. The Reverend Lew Rooker, then serving as pastor of Northern Light Church in Juneau, read a resolution passed by the Presbytery of Alaska. It read in part, "Whereas, some Presbyterian missionaries, with best intentions in bringing the gospel to Alaska, were among those who misunderstood the nature and purpose of Native [American] culture, art, and artifacts.... We disavow those teachings which led people to believe that abandoning Native [American] culture was a prerequisite for being Christian. We deeply regret the church's part in the destruction of Native [American] artifacts and the church's part in the loss of Native [American] languages."[3]

The ecumenical service included representatives of Lutheran, Catholic, and Russian Orthodox denominations. The two-hour service concluded with native representatives thanking the church people for their apologies. The native leaders said that the service had helped begin the healing of a deep pain.

The spiritual discipline of reconciliation not only helps us to heal the pains we have caused others, but also it helps us to begin experiencing God's healing in our own hearts and lives. Leonardo da Vinci experienced this lesson during his painting of *The Last Supper*.

According to tradition, da Vinci began this famous painting by portraying Judas with the face of a fellow artist. Leonardo da Vinci had experienced some hurt from the other painter and so wanted to vilify the fellow artist by portraying him as Judas. *The Last Supper* proceeded well until the final face was to be portrayed. For some reason da Vinci could not get the face of Jesus right. He kept starting over with the face of Christ. Finally, he realized that the problem was not with the paint or the topic, it was in his own heart. Leonardo da Vinci realized that he could not paint the face of Christ until he was reconciled with the fellow artist and had changed the face of Judas. Only after the other face was changed could he complete the painting with Christ's face.[4]

The first story in the recent book *Chicken Soup for the Christian Soul* is one by Corrie ten Boom. This amazing Dutch Christian participated in the underground railroad which helped Jews escape the Nazis during World War II. She and her family were captured and arrested for helping the Jews; her own sister and father died in Nazi concentration camps.

I heard Corrie ten Boom speak on the East Coast twenty years ago before she died. I recall that one of her illustrations of God's love and forgiveness was to say that God has removed our sins and cast them into the deepest sea. Then she smiled and said, "Then God places a sign out there that says, 'No Fishing Allowed.'" I recall that night the audience's bursting into applause. Corrie ten Boom's short story in *Chicken Soup for the Christian Soul* recounts the time that God forced her to live by her own words on reconciliation and forgiveness.

Shortly after the war ended, Corrie ten Boom began guest speaking in churches. One of her favorite topics was the need to be reconciled with the Germans who had supported the Nazi atrocities. In fact, she developed a ministry to help persecuted former Nazis just as she had once helped persecuted Jews. One evening, having used her familiar image of God's forgiveness and the need to stop fishing for past sins, she concluded her talk and watched a former Nazi guard come forward to speak with her. She immediately recognized him as one of the guards who had watched her and her sister undress and file past him during their time in the concentration camp at Ravensbruck.

The former Nazi complimented Corrie ten Boom on her talk and said that he particularly appreciated the idea that all our sins are forgiven by God. He told her that he had become a Christian since the war. He knew intellectually that Christianity offered complete forgiveness, but he still carried guilt feelings about his participation in the atrocities. Thus, he spoke to her about his need to feel forgiven by a former prisoner at Ravensbruck. He reached out to shake her hand as he asked her, "Fraulein will you forgive me?"

Corrie ten Boom recalls that she froze. It was one thing to believe that God has forgiven our sins, but it was another to actually forgive the man who had participated in her sister's death. Horrible memories of the concentration camp flooded back into her mind. Corrie ten Boom recalled how thin her sister was as she slowly deteriorated in health and finally died. She recalled the embarrassment of walking naked past this man and seeing her own sister's ribs standing out against her skin. Could she forgive him for the horrible death of her sister simply because he asked?

Corrie ten Boom recalled that it felt like hours to her as she pretended to be busy with her hand in her purse in order not to have to shake that former guard's hand. It was probably only a few seconds. She struggled to do the hardest thing she had ever done in her life. She wrestled with the realization that if she refused to forgive, she would simply be carrying her own bitterness at her own hurt. Knowing it was the right thing to do, more as an act of discipline than feeling, she asked the Lord to help her, praying, "Jesus help me! I can lift my hand. I can do that much. You supply the feeling." Then, she reached her hand out to shake the hand of her past persecutor.

And so woodenly, mechanically, I thrust my hand into the one stretched out to me. And as I did, an incredible thing took place. The current started in my shoulder, raced down my arm, and sprang into our joined hands. And then this healing warmth seemed to flood my whole being, bringing tears to my eyes.

"I forgive you brother!" I cried. "With all my heart."

For a long moment we grasped each other's hands—the former guard and the former prisoner. I had never known God's love so intensely as I did then.... It was the power of the Holy Spirit....[5]

Jesus wants to heal our broken relationships. The spiritual discipline of prayer is not enough to bring the healing Jesus wants to give. If we really want healing for ourselves and those we have hurt, we need to practice the spiritual discipline of reconciliation.

---

[1]V. Raymond Edman, *The Disciplines of Life* (Wheaton: VanKampen Press, 1948) Preface.

[2]This illustration came from the journal *Dynamic Preaching*, but I have lost the original source.

[3] "Apologies in Juneau," *Presbyterian Survey* January 1992: 35.

[4]Reprinted in *Dynamic Preaching*. Original illustration from sermon by Don Emmitte.

[5]Corrie ten Boom, "Love Your Enemy," *Chicken Soup for the Christian Soul* (Deerfield Beach: Health Communications, Inc., 1997) 4-5.

The Discipline of Evangelism

As he walked by the Sea of Galilee, he saw two brothers, Simon who is called Peter and Andrew his brother, casting a net into the sea; for they were fishermen. And he said to them, "Follow me, and I will make you fishers of men." Immediately they left their nets and followed him.

Matthew 4:18-20

And Jesus came and said to them, "All authority in heaven and on earth has been given to me. Go therefore and make disciples of all nations, baptizing them in the name of the Father and of the Son and of the Holy Spirit, teaching them to observe all that I have commanded you; and lo, I am with you always, to the close of the age."

Matthew 28:18-20

What would Jesus do? Would he proselytize? What comes to mind when we hear the word *proselytize*? Most of us think of an obnoxious preacher haranguing others on a street corner or Jehovah's Witnesses knocking on our door to tell us that their faith is right and that we are wrong. I do not believe that Jesus would proselytize. However, I do believe that Jesus would evangelize. What is the difference between evangelism and proselytism?

Last week we had visitors in our front yard. As I turned the corner, returning home from hiking, I spotted four Jehovah's Witnesses down the block coming in our direction. As I pulled into our driveway, I also saw a young man standing out at the curb, peering through the trees and bushes toward the front of our house. I suspected that Jehovah's Witnesses must be at our door, attempting to proselytize. I was not enthused about debating Jehovah's witnesses on my day off, so I was already considering my options for addressing our visitors. I was not ready for what met me on the walk to the door.

We had two javelina browsing in our front yard. The young man at the curb was watching these wild pigs with interest. Kathy and the children had been watching through the front window. Knowing that God works in mysterious ways, I wondered prayerfully if the two javelina had been sent by God to spare us from the Jehovah's Witnesses. To be honest, I would rather reason with javelina than to try and discuss the Scriptures with most Jehovah's Witnesses.

As you can guess, I do not agree with the Jehovah's Witnesses. I find their views alarming and non-Christian. The idea that God's name is Jehovah is one of the silliest ideas to come down the pike. For those in our church who do not know the origin of the word Jehovah, it comes from a blending of two Hebrew words. The consonants, *JHVH* come from the Hebrew word for *God*. It was considered so sacred to the Jews that it was never to be pronounced. Thus, there were no vowels, just four consonants. When the rabbis read the Scriptures, it became an interesting problem to determine how to read this word out loud to the congregation. The rabbis solved the problem by reading the Hebrew word for *Lord* whenever the Scriptures had the word *JHVH*. The result was that the Hebrew word *Adonay* came to be commonly read in place of the unpronounceable word for *God*. Eventually the word for *God* in the Hebrew Scriptures came to be written with the four consonants for *God, JHVH* and the three vowels from the word for *Lord, AOA*. In English the idea of combining the words for *Lord* and *God* might come out as *GORD* or *LOD*, which really mean nothing at all. In Hebrew the combination came out as JAHOVAH. It worked to protect God's unpronounceable name while reminding the rabbis to say *AdOnAy* out loud when reading Scriptures. To declare that this is God's real name is mere silliness.

I could take more time to argue against the Jehovah's Witness idea that Jesus is the same as the archangel Michael. I totally reject their misinterpretations of the Bible which lead them to believe that Jesus is a separate and lesser god. I could rant against their proselytism. However, in the midst of my strong disagreements with their doctrines, I have a great deal of respect for their discipline in telling others what they believe. Most of us are not as disciplined in our evangelism as they are in their proselytism.

Unfortunately many Christians have refused to take Jesus seriously when he called his followers to be "fishers of men." We have had a tendency to expect the local preacher or perhaps some professional evangelist such as Billy Graham to evangelize for us. We could learn a lesson from Jehovah's Witnesses. I think they are right in their interpretation of the Bible that Jesus intended all of his followers to practice the discipline of evangelism. This does not mean we have to go door to door, nor does it mean we must proselytize. What would it mean to practice evangelism as a spiritual discipline?

This summer our adult Sunday school class has been studying a series of lessons on evangelism. Through a combination of video presentations, small groups, and class discussions we have learned that disciplined evangelism involves a great deal of patience. We have recognized that many who do not believe in Jesus Christ have been turned off previously so that they have some significant barriers against the gospel. Unless we patiently befriend them and help them over the barriers, we will never see them come to faith in Christ. Evangelism, then, is a long, slow process of helping a person draw closer to Jesus Christ.

I cannot hope to summarize our twelve weeks of study and discussion in this one message. However, there are two points that are particularly worth remembering. First, one of the most comfortable and successful forms of evangelism is the sharing of our own faith journey. We do not need to preach at people in order to evangelize. We can help people discover who Jesus is and what he can do in their lives by sharing our own stories. One of the key differences between evangelism and proselytism is that proselytism preaches doctrines while evangelism tells a story.

When Kathy and I lived in a Tlinget Indian village in Alaska, we were struck by the way the native people would answer questions with a story. We would ask a fairly simple question and the native people would respond by launching into a story. If my question were about where to buy heating oil, the answer might involve a story about a tree's falling in the forest. If my question were about some church matter, an elder might respond with a story about a hunting trip.

I finally became comfortable enough with one of the elders in the village to ask why the native people almost always answered a question with a story. After telling me a story, he explained that it was considered rude in their culture to give direct advice or tell someone what to do. "You should do this, or you ought to do that," were considered insulting ways to tell someone something. Telling a story allows the listener to figure out the answer for himself. Thus, telling stories was considered the polite way to speak the truth.

Shakespeare used a wonderful example of storytelling in his famous play *Hamlet*. When young Hamlet learns from his father's ghost that his uncle murdered his father and usurped the throne, Hamlet wants to confront his uncle with the evil deed. Knowing that his uncle would deny it if he accused him directly, Hamlet comes up with a creative way to bring out the truth. He hires some traveling actors to perform a drama which includes a scene cleverly adapted by Hamlet himself. The scene involves a person who secretly commits murder in the same way that Hamlet's uncle murdered the king. As the hired actors perform the scene, Hamlet's uncle realizes that the scene is depicting the horrible crime he has committed. The uncle's reaction reveals his guilt.

A shared story has the ability to help people think about the parts of our lives which we do not want pried into by others. A story can reveal what is wrong without having to point fingers or claim that we are self-righteously better than others. In fact, frequently the best stories for evangelism are those which reveal with humor and honesty our own foibles and mistakes.

A pirate was walking down the street when a little boy stopped him. The boy stared at the pirate's peg leg, hook, and eye patch.

The boy asked, "Are you a real pirate?" The pirate nodded. "Is that peg leg real?" the boy queried. "Yes," the pirate replied, "it is." The boy asked, "How did you get a peg leg?" The pirate told him the story behind the leg.

"Well, son, I was battling this enemy ship when a cannon was shot at me. The cannonball hit me right in the knee and took off the bottom half of my leg. A friend made me this peg, and I've been using it ever since."

The boy was impressed. He continued his questioning of the pirate. "Is the hook real? How did you get the hook?" The pirate patiently responded with another story. "Well, it was like this. I was in a sword fight with another pirate. He beat me and cut off my right hand. A friend made me a hook to wear in place of the hand. I've been wearing this hook for years."

The boy was even more impressed than he had been about the peg leg. The boy then asked about the patch over one eye. "Are you really blind in that eye?" the boy asked. The pirate launched into another story. "One day I was out walking on the deck. It was such a beautiful day with the sky so clear that I looked up to admire the sky. Just as I was looking up, a bird flew over my head and pooped right into my eye."

The boy became skeptical. "I find it hard to believe that a little bird poop could put out your eye." The pirate responded, "It could when it's your first day with a hook for a hand!"

Our stories about our experiences do not have to be as dramatic as Hamlet's murder or a pirate's injuries to carry the truth of the gospel. In John 4, we read about a woman who met Jesus. She was at a well when Jesus arrived near her village. He asked her a few questions and then told her that he could offer her living water. When she discovered he was the Messiah, her life was turned around. The woman immediately headed back to her village and began telling her neighbors and friends what Jesus had done for her. They could hear the joy in her voice, and so they also went to meet Jesus. The gospel story ends with the rest of the people in her village discovering that Jesus could change their lives as well as hers.

While I grew up in a Christian home, I did not understand that Christianity involved letting Jesus take control of my life. I guess I thought being a Christian meant I had to try and be a good person. I thought that I was being a Christian as long as I went to church and gave some money in the Sunday school offering plate. My false concept of Christianity changed when I began attending a college Bible study group where people talked about Jesus in a whole new way. They spoke about him as though he were their personal friend. They prayed and talked with him in a tone of closeness which I had not known previously. As I listened to their stories of what Christ was doing in their lives, I began to want what they had.

I do not recall that they ever preached at me or made me feel less than Christian. I simply overheard their stories and knew that they were talking about something I did not have in my life. They never told me I was not a Christian; I made that discovery for myself by listening to their stories. Over the next months I came to the point where I wanted the relationship with Jesus Christ that I had heard them describe.

Evangelism is different from proselytism in that we do not have to point our fingers or condemn. We do not have to preach that someone else's doctrine is wrong. Instead, we simply tell our stories of what Christ has done for us, and they can listen to the stories and draw their own conclusions.

One of the members in our Sunday school class shared with me something exciting that happened to her during these classes. We took one of the class sessions to tell each other our faith stories. In small groups we told each other what God had done in our lives. I suggested that we practice sharing our faith stories so that we would feel less inhibited and more open to sharing them when an appropriate occasion arose in the future. The very next week one of our church members was invited by a neighbor to share how she had been able to keep going through some personal difficulties. In response she shared her faith story for the first time with her neighbor.

Sharing our faith stories is an important part of the spiritual discipline of evangelism. Anyone who has met Jesus Christ can learn to do this. A second aspect of the discipline of evangelism is the fact that we show our gospel to be relevant when we share our stories in nonreligious language. Our class was warned to avoid jargon phrases which are unfamiliar and uncomfortable for non-Christians.

I first discovered this idea some years ago when I was learning about the Twelve Steps used in recovery programs. The founder of the Oxford Groups, from which the Twelve Steps grew, used to remind the Christians in his Bible study groups to use "pagan language" when sharing their faith stories. He taught them to, "Avoid pious phraseology, and talk in the language that Pagans understand."[1]

Some years ago I was working on a sermon on the reason that the Twelve Step movements had grown in comparison to the churches. I was researching and reading a book on the history of the Twelve Step movements. The morning I was reading the book, I kept being interrupted by the telephone. Finally, I took my notes and book and told the secretary I was staying away from the office until I had my sermon composed.

I went to a local restaurant, ordered a pastry and some coffee, and settled in to read the chapter on the history of Twelve Step evangelism. I had just finished reading the chapter, taking notes, and was eating my pastry when I overheard a conversation coming from the booth next to me. I could not see the two men, but I picked up from their discussion that they were construction workers. The first guy said, "I've really messed up my life." Okay, he didn't actually use the word *messed* but a four-letter word which communicated how disastrous his situation had been. He went on, "My life was ruined because of my problem with alcohol." With colorful language he told his story about how drinking had ruined his marriage. Then he said, "You know what? I found out about this group that uses these Twelve Steps. They told me about this Higher Power stuff." Okay, he didn't use the word *stuff*. He used a four-letter word, but I knew what he meant.

I listened to this construction worker use raw street language as he told about how a Higher Power and Twelve Steps had changed his life. I was amazed that God had given me such a direct experience of evangelism using the language that his friend would understand. When I prepared to leave, I noticed the other person was intently listening to the story. What an example of evangelism!

I am not saying that we must use four-letter words to practice the discipline of evangelism. I am showing that we need to use the language which is meaningful for those we want to reach. For some of us it may mean telling our faith story with images taken from music. Others may use sports images to describe our lives. Still others may speak in the language of the cultured and educated in order to reach those who need the gospel in their native tongue. It all depends on our own culture and those to whom God has called us to witness.

If we want to follow in the footsteps of Jesus and do what he would do, we must learn the spiritual discipline of evangelism. Jesus' last words as he departed this world were about carrying his message to the entire world. If we wait until they come to church, they will be lost. If we insist that people clean up their lives and be good, moral people before they can become Christians, we have failed to do what Jesus did.

The Reverend King Duncan is an editor of a magazine called *Dynamic Preaching*. He frequently is invited to guest preach at various churches. Some years ago he wrote about an experience he had on a Sunday morning as he was preparing to guest preach in a historic, downtown church. The church had put him in a nice hotel room for the Saturday night before he was scheduled to preach. The congregation consisted of several wealthy members. They prided themselves on their huge, beautiful, well-maintained sanctuary. While dressing in the hotel room on that Sunday morning, King Duncan flipped on the radio and heard a Pentecostal preacher broadcasting from a local church. What caught his attention as he started to button up his shirt was listening to the radio preacher lecturing his congregation. The preacher said, "Now, before I start my sermon, I want to say something. Quit fidgeting and moving around all the time while I'm preaching. It distracts me. How do you expect me to preach when you are always squirming and moving all the time during the service? Surely you can sit still for a worship service!"

King Duncan began to laugh. He thought to himself, "I can't believe this preacher is saying this over the radio!" Then the preacher continued his harangue. "I'm going to say something else! You can wait until the end of the sermon before you go to the bathroom! I have to wait until I finish my sermon. You can too! You can go to the bathroom before you come into this service, wait until the end of the service, and then go to the bathroom again. If I can last, you can last." Reverend Duncan thought he would die laughing. Here was a preacher lecturing his congregation on politeness and manners.

In the midst of his laughter King Duncan felt the Spirit of God whispering to his conscience. The Spirit of God said, "King, the reason that pastor has to tell his people how to behave in church is that a year ago many of them were not in a church. Some of them were having serious problems with alcohol and drugs. Some of them were going through painful divorces. A few were even in jail. This is why they do not know how to act in church. They have not been in church very long." Then God said, "Don't worry, King, you won't have that difficulty at old First Church."[2]

Do you want to know one of the signs of a dying church? Everybody in the sanctuary knows how to act. Everybody in worship knows when to stand and when to sit. Everybody has the *Doxology* and *Gloria Patri* memorized. Nobody mistakes "debts" with "transgressions" in the Lord's Prayer. Show me this kind of church, and I will show you a dying church!

Let us pray, as we seek to do what Jesus would do, that we may faithfully evangelize those who have not yet met our Lord. May we be ready to tell our stories of what God has done and is doing in our lives. May we speak the language of those to whom God has called us to witness.

---

[1] A.J. Russell, *For Sinners Only* (New York: Harper & Bros., 1932) 81.

[2] King Duncan, *Dynamic Preaching* February 1992: 12.